The Great Holiday Baking Book

The Great Holiday Baking Book: Copyright © 2011
by Northland Aluminum Products, Inc. and CulinartMedia, Inc.

Published by
Northland Aluminum Products, Inc.
NORDIC WARE and BUNDT BAKEWARE
5005 Highway 7
Minneapolis, MN 55416

Produced by
CulinartMedia, Inc.
169 Port Road, Suite 41
Kennebunk, ME 04043

Editors: Reed Winter, Shannon Mahoney and Susan Stover
Design: Harrah Lord
Photo Credits: Eising Food Photography
    Claudia Ross Tjornhom, pages 34 & 42
Layout: Patty Holden
Recipe Testing: Julie Stanton

ISBN 978-0-9744605-0

Printed in the USA by RR Donnelley

𝒩𝑜𝑟𝒹𝒾𝒸 𝒲𝒶𝓇ℯ products have become a central icon in many American kitchens. In fact, every 4.5 seconds a Nordic Ware product is purchased somewhere in the world. Over 60 million Bundt® pans are in use, and the number continues to grow with an extensive new line of Bundt® shapes added in recent years.

Founded by H. David and Dorothy Dalquist in 1946, Nordic Ware remains family-owned and dedicated to providing outstanding customer service and support for their great innovative kitchenware products. Nordic Ware's commitment to inventing and re-inventing its line of American-made cookware, bakeware, microwave and barbeque products is paralleled only by the company's commitment to the community, its customers and employees and maintaining a "family" atmosphere. Customer satisfaction and loyalty are the basis for Nordic Ware's continued success. The company has stood the test of time from its inception in 1946, to its recent transition from middle class marvel to gourmet comfort food status.

Although the company's first products were ethnic bakeware products such as the Rosette Iron, Ebleskiver Pan and Krumkake Iron, Nordic Ware is best known for its Bundt® Pan. It was after a large baking competition in 1966 where the winning recipe, the Tunnel of Fudge cake, was baked in a Bundt Pan, that the popularity of the Bundt Pan among the general public skyrocketed.

With **The Great HOLIDAY BAKING Book**, Nordic Ware is pleased to present a collection of family-tested recipes that have withstood the test of time. Who can't recall the anticipation of warm holiday treats fresh from the oven, fingers covered with a dusting of powdered sugar and sneaking a spoonful of batter or cookie dough? Nearly everyone can recall fond memories of time spent baking with their families. Many of the recipes in this book are kid-friendly for full family participation during baking. All of the recipes in this book can be made with a few simple items found in every kitchen and ingredients from your local grocer. Happy baking!

contents

cakes

8 Black Forest Cake

10 Holiday Bundt Cake

12 Double Chocolate Torte

14 Chocolate Raspberry Tartlets

16 Maple Walnut Bundt Cake

17 Spiced Almond Crunch Bundt Cake

19 Chocolate Layer Cake

20 Chocolate Cherry Gift

21 Dark Fruit Cake

22 Gingerbread House Bundt Cake

24 Festive Mocha Cake

26 Orange Spice Cranberry Chocolate Bundt Cake

29 Dark Chocolate Raspberry Cake

30 Chocolate Vanilla Village

31 Layered Gateau with Berries

32 Cherry Cream-Filled Sponge Cake Roll

34 Holiday Honey Torte

cookies

36 Brownie Trees

38 White Chocolate Clusters

39 Soft and Chewy Sugar Cookies

40 Crisp and Delicate Sugar Cookies

42 Holiday Mouse Cookies

43 Decorated Pecan Cookies

45 Pistachio Butter Cookies with Chocolate Hazelnut Filling

46 Bear Paw Cookies

48 Peanut Blossoms

49 Chocolate Turtle Cookies

51 Hazelnut Brownies with White Chocolate Frosting

52 Pecan Triangles

53 Chocolate Pinwheel Cookies

54 Almond Meringues with Chocolate Drizzle

56 Cranberry White Chocolate Macadamia Cookies

58 Rum Truffles

holiday specialties

59 Chocolate Peppermint Candies

60 Vanilla Peppermint Cupcakes

62 Chocolate Bark with Cranberries and Pistachios

63 Cinnamon Mini-Muffins

65 Tree-Shaped Dinner Rolls

66 Peppermint Meringues

67 Pecan Sticky Buns

68 Glazed Orange Cupcakes with Sugared Cranberries

70 Pudding Truffles

71 Ice Cream and Coconut Snowmen

73 Blackberry and Raspberry Tart

74 Dark Chocolate Truffles

75 Walnut Potica

76 Julbullar Swedish Sweet Rolls

78 Glazed Walnut Stollen

79 Gift Fruit Cakes

80 Meringue Rosettes with Coffee Cream

cakes

Black Forest Cake

ingredients ❊

for glazed cherries

2½ cups (450 g) canned pitted cherries,
    drained (reserve juice)

2 tablespoons kirsch or cherry brandy

1 tablespoon cornstarch

for sponge cake

6 large eggs, room temperature

1 cup (200 g) sugar

1 teaspoon vanilla extract

½ cup (60 g) all-purpose flour, sifted

½ cup (45 g) unsweetened cocoa powder

⅔ cup (160 g) unsalted butter, melted (1⅓ sticks)

for syrup

⅔ cup (65 g) sugar

½ cup (120 ml) water

3 tablespoons kirsch

for filling

3 cups (720 ml) heavy cream

½ cup (60 g) confectioners' sugar

2 packets cream stabilizer (such as Whip It)

1 teaspoon vanilla extract

16 drained canned cherries, from above

7 ounces (200 g) bittersweet chocolate, grated

for glazed cherries

1. Set aside 16 cherries for garnish. Combine remaining cherries with kirsch and let stand for 1 hour.

2. In a small saucepan, mix cornstarch with ⅔ cup (160 ml) reserved cherry juice. Bring to a boil, reduce heat and simmer 5 minutes or until thickened, stirring constantly. Let cool, add kirsch soaked cherries and stir well. Set aside.

for sponge cake

1. Grease and lightly flour 3 round 8-inch (20 cm) cake pans. Preheat oven to 350°F (180°C).

2. In a large bowl, using an electric mixer on high speed, beat eggs until light and fluffy. Gradually add sugar, beating well. Beat until very thick, about 10 minutes. Add vanilla.

3. Sift flour and cocoa powder together. Fold into egg mixture in 4 additions. Fold in melted butter, in 4 additions until well combined. Gently pour into prepared pans. Bake for 15 minutes or until the center of the cake springs back when lightly touched.

4. Cool in the pans for 5 minutes on wire racks. Remove from pans and cool completely.

for syrup

In a small saucepan over medium heat, stir sugar and water together until sugar dissolves. Bring to a boil and boil for 5 minutes. Cool and stir in kirsch.

for filling and to assemble

1. Using a wooden skewer, make holes in the tops of each cake. Drizzle syrup over the cakes. Let sit.

2. Beat heavy cream with confectioners' sugar until peaks form. Beat in 2 packets of cream stabilizer. Add vanilla and beat until stiff peaks form.

3. Invert one cake layer onto a cake plate. Spread with glazed cherries and 1 cup (60 g) of whipped cream. Top with second cake layer, spread 1 cup (60 g) whipped cream evenly over the top.

4. Add top cake layer. Spread whipped cream over the sides and top of the cake, reserving some whipped cream for rosettes. Spoon remaining whipped cream into a pastry bag. Pipe 16 rosettes around the top of the cake. Top each with a cherry. Refrigerate cake for at least 1 hour.

5. Before serving, sprinkle grated chocolate around the sides of the cake and in the center. Serve.

Holiday Bundt Cake

❄ 12 SERVINGS

PREP TIME: 20 MIN
BAKING TIME: 50–55 MIN

ingredients ❄ ❄ ❄ ❄ ❄ ❄ ❄ ❄ ❄

for cake

⅔ cup (100 g) raisins

3 tablespoons rum

4 cups (480 g) all-purpose flour

2 teaspoons baking powder

¼ teaspoon salt

¼ teaspoon ground cloves

½ teaspoon cinnamon

1⅛ cups (270 g) unsalted butter, softened
    (2¼ sticks)

1⅛ cups (225 g) sugar

6 large eggs

1 teaspoon vanilla extract

½ cup (120 ml) milk

1 tablespoon lemon zest, grated

for glaze and decorating

5 tablespoons (75 g) unsalted butter, melted

2 cups (240 g) confectioners' sugar

1½ teaspoons vanilla extract

2–4 tablespoons milk

1 bottle green cookie icing

½ cup (85 g) red chocolate buttons,
    (such as M & M® candies)

method ❄ ❄ ❄ ❄ ❄ ❄ ❄ ❄ ❄

for cake

1. In a small bowl, stir raisins with rum and soak for 1 hour.

2. Preheat oven to 350°F (180°C). Spray a Bundt pan with baking spray or grease and dust lightly with flour, tapping out any excess.

3. In a large bowl, sift flour, baking powder, salt and spices together. Set aside.

4. In a separate bowl, using an electric mixer on medium speed, beat butter and sugar together until light and creamy. Beat in 1 egg at a time, mixing well. Scrape sides of the bowl and add vanilla.

5. Reduce mixer speed to low. Add flour mixture in thirds, alternating with the milk, and ending with flour. Fold in the rum-soaked raisins and lemon zest.

6. Pour batter into prepared Bundt pan. Bake for 50 to 60 minutes, until a cake tester inserted near the center comes out clean. Cool in the pan for 10 minutes on a wire rack. Invert onto rack and cool completely.

for glaze and decorating

1. In a mixing bowl, combine melted butter, confectioners' sugar and vanilla. Slowly add milk, 1 tablespoon at a time to thin. Mix until smooth. Drizzle glaze over completely cooled cake.

2. Make holly boughs using ready-made green icing. Use M & M candies for berries. Allow icing to set. Serve.

Double Chocolate Torte

❄ 16 SERVINGS

PREP TIME: 30 MIN
COOKING TIME: 50 MIN
CHILLING TIME: 6–8 HR

ingredients ❊

for crust

1½ cups (165 g) graham cracker crumbs,
    finely ground

⅓ cup (65 g) sugar

6 tablespoons (90 g) unsalted butter, melted
    (¾ stick)

for cake

8 ounces (230 g) semisweet chocolate, chopped

1 cup (240 g) unsalted butter (2 sticks)

1 cup (200 g) sugar

5 large eggs, room temperature

1 teaspoon vanilla extract

¼ cup (30 g) all-purpose flour

¼ teaspoon salt

for mousse

½ cup (120 g) unsalted butter, cubed (1 stick)

4 large eggs, separated

¼ cup (60 ml) heavy cream

2 teaspoons vanilla extract

8 ounces (230 g) semisweet chocolate, chopped

½ cup (100 g) sugar

for crème anglaise

1 cup (240 ml) heavy cream

¼ cup (50 g) sugar

1 teaspoon vanilla extract

3 egg yolks, beaten

48 fresh raspberries

Fresh mint

Cocoa powder

method ❋

for crust

In a small bowl, mix graham cracker crumbs, sugar and melted butter together until well blended. Press mixture into the bottom of a 10-inch (23 cm) springform pan. Set aside.

for cake

1. Preheat oven to 325°F (170°C). Melt chocolate and butter in a large saucepan over low heat, stirring constantly. Remove from heat and let cool. Whisk in sugar. Add 1 egg at a time, stirring well after each egg. Add vanilla, flour and salt.

2. Pour mixture on top of the graham cracker crust. Bake until the cake rises in the center, about 35 minutes. Do not overcook—tester will not come out clean. Cool completely in the pan on a wire rack. Cover and refrigerate while preparing mousse.

for mousse

1. Melt butter in the top half of a double boiler set over simmering water. In a separate bowl, whisk 4 egg yolks, cream and vanilla to blend. Gradually whisk egg yolk mixture into the melted butter. Whisk over simmering water for about 6 minutes or until an instant-read thermometer reaches 150°F (65°C).

2. Remove from heat, add chocolate and stir to melt. Set aside.

3. Using an electric mixer on high speed, beat 4 egg whites and sugar in a large bowl until stiff peaks form. Add one quarter of the egg white mixture to the warm chocolate mixture and whisk to blend. Fold in the remaining eggs whites. Pour mousse mixture over the cake in the pan, smoothing top. Chill until mousse is set, at least 6 hours or overnight.

for crème anglaise

1. In a medium saucepan, combine the cream, sugar and vanilla. Bring mixture to a gentle boil over medium-low heat. Immediately remove pan from heat.

2. In a separate bowl, whisk 3 egg yolks to blend. Whisk half of the warm cream into the egg yolks. Return mixture to the saucepan and cook for about 5 minutes or until mixture has thickened, stirring constantly.

3. Strain into bowl. Cover and refrigerate until completely chilled.

to serve

1. Run a sharp knife around the edge of the springform pan to loosen. Release the sides of the pan.

2. Place sliced torte on serving plates. Garnish with fresh raspberries and mint sprigs. Drizzle crème anglaise over torte and raspberries. Dust with cocoa powder. Serve.

Chocolate Raspberry Tartlets

❄ 24 SERVINGS

PREP TIME: 30 MIN
CHILLING TIME: 1 HR
BAKING TIME: 15 MIN

ingredients ❄ ❄ ❄ ❄ ❄ ❄ ❄ ❄ ❄ ❄

for pastry tart shells

2½ cups (300 g) all-purpose flour, plus extra
⅔ cup (80 g) confectioners' sugar
¼ teaspoon salt
1¼ cups (300 g) unsalted butter, chilled (2½ sticks)
4 egg yolks, beaten with 2 tablespoons water

for chocolate pastry cream

3 egg yolks
¼ cup (50 g) sugar
2 tablespoons all-purpose flour
2 tablespoons cornstarch
1¼ cup (300 ml) milk
1 teaspoon vanilla extract
¼ cup (60 ml) heavy cream
½ cup (100 g) milk chocolate, chopped

48 fresh raspberries
48 almond slivers
Confectioners' sugar, for dusting

method ❄ ❄ ❄ ❄ ❄ ❄ ❄ ❄ ❄ ❄

for pastry tart shells

1. In the bowl of a food processor, combine flour, sugar and salt. Pulse to mix. Cut butter into pieces, add and pulse for 20 seconds or until pea-size crumbs form. While pulsing, add the egg yolk and water mixture. Pulse until large, moist crumbs form. Do not over process.

2. Place dough on a lightly floured work surface. Divide into quarters and shape each piece into a flat 5-inch (13 cm) disc. Wrap each in plastic wrap and refrigerate for 1 hour or more.

3. Position oven rack in the center of the oven. Preheat oven to 375°F (190°C).

4. Working with 1 dough disc at a time, roll to ¼-inch (.5 cm) thickness. Using a round 3-inch (7.5 cm) cutter, cut out 24 pieces. Place each in a mini-muffin pan. Press the dough into each well, trimming if needed.

5. Bake for about 15 minutes, until the pastry shells are crisp and golden. Cool in the pan for 5 minutes on a wire rack. Remove shells from pan carefully and cool on rack.

for chocolate pastry cream

1. In a medium bowl, whisk egg yolks with sugar, flour and cornstarch. Set aside.

2. In a small saucepan over medium-high heat, bring milk to a boil. Slowly stir ¼ cup (60 ml) hot milk into the egg mixture. Add egg mixture back into the saucepan and cook over low heat stirring constantly, until thick as pudding. Add vanilla and stir. Remove from heat.

3. In a small saucepan heat the cream and chopped chocolate over medium heat. Stir until the chocolate is melted and smooth.

4. Stir the chocolate mixture into the thickened pastry cream. Let cool and cover with plastic wrap pressed against the chocolate cream and refrigerate.

to assemble

Fill each shell with 1½ tablespoons of chilled chocolate cream filling. Garnish each with 2 raspberries. Place an almond sliver between the berries and dust with confectioners' sugar. Serve.

Maple Walnut Bundt Cake

❄ 12 SERVINGS

PREP TIME: 20 MIN
BAKING TIME: 50 MIN

ingredients ❋ ❋ ❋ ❋ ❋ ❋ ❋ ❋ ❋ ❋ ❋

for cake

2½ cups (300 g) all-purpose flour
2 teaspoons baking soda
2 teaspoons baking powder
½ teaspoon cinnamon
½ teaspoon salt
½ cup (120 g) unsalted butter, softened (1 stick)
½ cup (100 g) sugar
2 large eggs
1 cup (240 ml) pure maple syrup
1½ teaspoons vanilla extract
½ cup (120 ml) milk
1 cup (120 g) walnuts, finely chopped

for maple frosting

1½ cups (180 g) confectioners' sugar
¼ cup (60 ml) pure maple syrup
1 tablespoon milk
3 tablespoons unsalted butter, softened

6 walnut halves, for garnish

method ❋ ❋ ❋ ❋ ❋ ❋ ❋ ❋ ❋ ❋

for cake

1. Preheat the oven to 350°F (180°C). Spray a Bundt pan with baking spray or grease and dust lightly with flour, tapping out any excess.

2. In a medium bowl, sift flour, baking soda, baking powder, cinnamon and salt together. Set aside.

3. In a large bowl, using an electric mixer on high speed, beat butter and sugar together until light and creamy. Beat in 1 egg at a time, mixing well. Scrap sides of the bowl and add the maple syrup and vanilla.

4. Reduce mixer speed to low. Add flour mixture in thirds, alternating with the milk and ending with flour mixture. Fold in the walnuts.

5. Pour batter into prepared Bundt pan. Bake for 50 minutes or until a cake tester inserted near the center comes out clean. Cool in the pan for 10 minutes on a wire rack. Invert onto rack and cool completely.

for maple frosting

In a mixing bowl, combine confectioners' sugar, maple syrup, milk and butter. Mix until creamy. Smooth over completely cooled cake. Garnish with walnut halves. Serve.

Spiced Almond Crunch Bundt Cake

❄ 12 SERVINGS

PREP TIME: 30 MIN
BAKING TIME: 55–60 MIN

ingredients ✳ ✳ ✳ ✳ ✳ ✳ ✳ ✳ ✳ ✳

1 cup (140 g) blanched almonds

2¼ cups (450 g) sugar, divided

2 tablespoons water

3 cups (360 g) all-purpose flour

1 teaspoon cinnamon

¼ teaspoon ground ginger

¼ teaspoon ground nutmeg

1½ teaspoon baking powder

½ teaspoon salt

1⅛ cups (270 g) unsalted butter, softened
    (2¼ sticks)

5 large eggs, room temperature

1 teaspoon vanilla extract

1 cup (240 ml) milk, warmed

½ cup (120 ml) pure maple syrup

Confectioners' sugar, for garnish

Decorative candies, for garnish

method ✳ ✳ ✳ ✳ ✳ ✳ ✳ ✳ ✳ ✳

1. Preheat oven to 325°F (170°C). Spray a Bundt pan with baking spray or grease and dust lightly with flour, tapping out any excess.

2. For the filling: melt ½ cup (100 g) sugar with 2 tablespoons of water in a heavy saucepan until dissolved. Boil until the syrup darkens around the edges. Swirl the pan and cook until it turns a deep amber color. Remove from heat, add almonds and stir well. Pour onto a greased baking sheet and let cool. Chop caramelized almonds coarsely and set aside.

3. In a large bowl, sift flour, spices, baking powder and salt together. Set aside.

4. Using an electric mixer on medium speed, beat butter and remaining sugar until smooth and creamy, about 4 minutes. Beat in 1 egg at a time, mixing well after each egg. Scrape sides of the bowl and add vanilla.

5. Reduce mixer speed to low. Add flour mixture in thirds, alternating with the milk and ending with flour mixture. Beat for about 30 seconds, until batter is smooth.

6. Pour a third of the batter into the Bundt pan. Sprinkle with half the caramelized almonds. Pour in another third of the batter and sprinkle with remaining almonds. Pour in the remaining batter.

7. Bake for 55 to 60 minutes, until a cake tester inserted near the center comes out clean. Cool in the pan for 15 minutes on a wire rack. Invert onto rack and cool completely.

8. In a saucepan, reduce maple syrup by half and brush onto the cake. Let cake cool completely before serving. Garnish with confectioners' sugar and candies.

[BAKED IN THE NORDIC WARE HOLIDAY TREE PAN]

cakes

Chocolate Layer Cake

PREP TIME: 45 MIN
BAKING TIME: 30–35 MIN
CHILLING TIME: 1 HR

ingredients ✳ ✳ ✳ ✳ ✳ ✳ ✳ ✳ ✳ ✳

for cake

1½ cups (360 g) unsalted butter, softened (3 sticks)
1½ cups (300 g) sugar
6 large eggs, room temperature
2¼ cups (270 g) all-purpose flour
6 tablespoons (30 g) unsweetened cocoa powder
2 teaspoons baking powder
2 teaspoons vanilla extract
½ cup (50 g) almonds, finely ground
½ cup (120 ml) boiling water

for chocolate frosting

6 tablespoons (90 g) unsalted butter
7 ounces (200 g) semisweet chocolate, chopped
2 large eggs
1⅔ cups (200 g) confectioners' sugar

for chocolate curls and decorating

1 block chocolate, room temperature
½ cup (85 g) mini-chocolate chips
Confectioners' sugar, for dusting
Marzipan figure (optional)

method ✳ ✳ ✳ ✳ ✳ ✳ ✳ ✳ ✳ ✳

for cake

1. Preheat oven to 350°F (180°C). Line the bottoms of 2 round 9-inch (23 cm) cake pans with parchment paper. Grease the sides of the pans.

2. Beat the softened butter and sugar together until light and fluffy. Add 1 egg at a time, mixing well after each egg.

3. Sift flour, cocoa powder and baking powder together. Add to the butter mixture with the vanilla and finely ground almonds. Add boiling water and mix well.

4. Divide batter into prepared pans. Bake for 30 to 35 minutes, until a cake tester inserted into the centers comes out with a few moist crumbs attached. Cool in the pans for 10 minutes on a wire rack. Invert onto rack and cool completely.

for chocolate frosting

1. Melt butter and chopped chocolate in the top of a double boiler. Remove from heat.

2. Beat the eggs with confectioners' sugar and mix well with the chocolate and butter mixture.

3. Use one third of the frosting to sandwich the two cake layers together. Using a cake spatula, coat the cake with the remaining frosting to a smooth finish.

for chocolate curls and decorating

1. Have the block of chocolate at room temperature. Holding a chef's knife at a 45° angle, drag the knife across the top of the block of chocolate. This will create a long curl of chocolate. Place curls on top of the cake in 3 overlapping layers. Decorate the bottom of the cake with mini-chocolate chips.

2. Refrigerate the cake to set frosting. Remove from refrigerator 1 to 2 hours before serving. Dust the top of the cake lightly with confectioners' sugar. Place marzipan figure in center, if desired.

Chocolate Cherry Gift

❄ 10 SERVINGS

PREP TIME: 20 MIN
BAKING TIME: 35–40 MIN

ingredients ❋ ❋ ❋ ❋ ❋ ❋ ❋ ❋ ❋ ❋

1¾ cups (210 g) all-purpose flour
1 teaspoon baking powder
¼ teaspoon salt
½ cup (120 g) unsalted butter, softened (1 stick)
½ cup (100 g) sugar
1 teaspoon vanilla extract
2 large eggs, room temperature
3 ounces (90 g) semisweet chocolate, chopped
½ cup (120 ml) heavy cream
½ cup (60 g) dried cherries, chopped
Colored sugar, for garnish

method ❋ ❋ ❋ ❋ ❋ ❋ ❋ ❋ ❋ ❋

1. Preheat oven to 325°F (170°C). Spray Bundt pan with baking spray or grease and dust lightly with flour, tapping out any excess.

2. In a bowl, sift flour, baking powder and salt together. Set aside.

3. Using an electric mixer on medium speed, beat butter and sugar until smooth and creamy, about 4 minutes. Add vanilla. Beat in 1 egg at a time, mixing well. Scrape sides of the bowl after each addition.

4. Melt chocolate in a microwave safe bowl on medium for 1 to 2 minutes. Stir until melted and stir into butter mixture. Gradually stir in flour mixture and cream.

5. Pour a third of the batter into the Bundt pan. Sprinkle with half the cherries. Pour in another third of the batter and sprinkle with remaining cherries. Pour in the remaining batter.

6. Bake for 35 to 40 minutes. Cool in the pan for 10 minutes on a wire rack. Invert onto rack and cool completely.

7. Garnish with colored sugar.

[BAKED IN THE NORDIC WARE PRETTY PRESENTS PAN]

Dark Fruit Cake

❄ 12 SERVINGS

PREP TIME: 25 MIN
BAKING TIME: 1 HR–1 HR 10 MIN

ingredients ✳ ✳ ✳ ✳ ✳ ✳ ✳ ✳ ✳ ✳

½ cup (70 g) raisins
½ cup (75 g) dates, chopped
½ cup (75 g) candied cherries, chopped
2 tablespoons bourbon
1 cup (240 g) unsalted butter, softened (2 sticks)
1 cup (220 g) brown sugar, firmly packed
2 large eggs
⅓ cup (80 ml) molasses
1 cup (250 g) applesauce
1 cup (240 g) blackberry jam
1¾ cups (210 g) all-purpose flour
½ cup (60 g) whole wheat flour
1 teaspoon baking soda
2 teaspoons cinnamon
½ teaspoon ground nutmeg
½ teaspoon allspice
½ teaspoon cloves
1 cup (120 g) walnuts, chopped
4 tablespoons bourbon, optional
Sliced fruit, optional garnish

method ✳ ✳ ✳ ✳ ✳ ✳ ✳ ✳ ✳ ✳

1. In a bowl, combine raisins, dates and cherries with bourbon. Rest for 1 hour, stirring occasionally.

2. Preheat oven to 375°F (190°C). Spray Bundt pan with baking spray and dust lightly with flour, tapping out any excess.

3. In a large bowl, cream butter and sugar together until light and fluffy. In another bowl, beat eggs and combine with molasses, applesauce and blackberry jam. Slowly add the egg mixture to the butter mixture, mixing thoroughly.

4. Sift the flours, baking soda and spices into the wet mixture, mixing to combine. Fold in the fruit mixture and the walnuts and stir to blend.

5. Spoon the batter into the Bundt pan and bake for 60 to 70 minutes, until a cake tester inserted near the center comes out clean.

6. Cool in the pan for 10 minutes on a wire rack. Invert onto rack and cool completely. Drizzle the top with bourbon if desired. Garnish with sliced fruit to serve.

Gingerbread House Bundt Cake

ingredients ❄ ❄ ❄ ❄ ❄ ❄ ❄ ❄ ❄ ❄

for cake

2½ cups (300 g) all-purpose flour

1 teaspoon cinnamon

1 teaspoon ground ginger

¼ teaspoon ground nutmeg

⅛ teaspoon ground cloves

⅛ teaspoon ground cardamom

1½ teaspoon baking powder

¼ teaspoon salt

1 cup (240 g) unsalted butter, softened (2 sticks)

1½ (300 g) cups sugar

4 large eggs, room temperature

1 teaspoon vanilla extract

1 cup (240 ml) milk, warmed

for icing

5 tablespoons (75 g) unsalted butter, melted

2 cups (240 g) confectioners' sugar, plus extra

1½ teaspoons vanilla extract

2–4 tablespoons milk

Confectioners' sugar
Mini marshmallows
Gumdrops

method ❄ ❄ ❄ ❄ ❄ ❄ ❄ ❄ ❄ ❄

for cake

1. Preheat oven to 325°F (170°C). Spray Bundt pan with baking spray or grease and dust lightly with flour, tapping out any excess.

2. In a large bowl, sift flour, cinnamon, ginger, nutmeg, cloves, cardamom, baking powder and salt together. Set aside.

3. Using an electric mixer on medium speed, beat butter and sugar together until smooth and creamy, about 4 minutes. Beat in 1 egg at a time. Scrape sides of the bowl after each egg. Beat in vanilla.

4. Reduce mixer speed to low. Add flour mixture in thirds alternating with the milk, and ending with flour mixture.

5. Pour batter into prepared Bundt pan. Bake for 50 to 55 minutes until a cake tester inserted into the center comes out clean. Cool in the pan for 10 minutes on a wire rack. Invert onto rack and cool completely before decorating.

for icing

In a mixing bowl, combine melted butter, confectioners' sugar and vanilla. Slowly add milk, 1 tablespoon at a time and mix until smooth. Use icing to decorate cake. Decorate with confectioners' sugar, marshmallows and gumdrops.

[BAKED IN THE NORDIC WARE GINGERBREAD HOUSE PAN]

Festive Mocha Cake

❄ 12 SERVINGS

PREP TIME: 35 MIN
BAKING TIME: 30–35 MIN
CHILLING TIME: 2 HR

for cake

4 large eggs, separated
⅔ cup (130 g) sugar
1 teaspoon vanilla extract
1 cup (140 g) cake flour
¼ cup (25 g) ground almonds
2 teaspoons baking powder

for filling and buttercream frosting

4 large eggs

1 cup (200 g) sugar

¼ teaspoon salt

2 cups (480 g) unsalted butter, softened but cool (4 sticks)

2 tablespoons instant coffee

2 tablespoons warm water

1 tablespoon rum

3–4 tablespoons orange marmalade

to decorate

Cocoa powder, for dusting

Coffee beans

Chocolate toffee candy bar bits (such as Heath®)

Decorative chocolate hearts and lattice, optional

method ✳ ✳ ✳ ✳ ✳ ✳ ✳ ✳ ✳ ✳

for cake

1. Preheat oven to 350°F (180°C). Grease a 10-inch (25 cm) springform pan and dust lightly with flour, tapping out any excess.

2. Beat egg whites, sugar and vanilla together until stiff peaks form. In a separate bowl, combine egg yolks, flour, ground almonds and baking powder, mixing until blended. Gently fold in the egg whites.

3. Pour batter into prepared pan and smooth the top. Bake for 30 to 35 minutes, until a cake tester inserted in the middle comes out clean. Cool in the pan for 10 minutes on a wire rack. Release cake from pan and cool completely.

for filling and buttercream frosting

1. In a heatproof bowl, combine the eggs, sugar and salt. Place the bowl over, not in a pan of simmering water. Whisking constantly, heat the mixture to 160°F (70°C) on an instant-read thermometer. Mixture will be foamy and thin. Remove from heat.

2. Using an electric mixer on medium-high speed, beat the egg mixture for about 5 minutes until light, fluffy and cooled to room temperature.

3. Cut each stick of butter into quarters. Reduce mixer speed to medium and add butter 1 piece at a time to egg mixture. Dissolve coffee in warm water and add the rum. Slowly add to the buttercream. Increase mixer speed to high and beat for about 1 minute, until frosting is light and fluffy and blended.

to assemble and decorate

1. Carefully cut cooled cake horizontally into 3 layers. Spread orange marmalade on the bottom layer. Place the middle layer on top and spread the middle layer with a quarter of the buttercream frosting. Place on the top layer and cover the entire cake with the remaining frosting.

2. Dust the bottom of the cake with cocoa powder. Decorate the top of the cake with swirls of cocoa powder, coffee beans and toffee bits. Surround the cake with prepared chocolate hearts and place chocolate lattice in the center of the cake, if using.

3. Refrigerate for 1 to 2 hours before serving.

Orange Spice Cranberry Chocolate Bundt Cake

※ 12 SERVINGS

PREP TIME: 20 MIN
BAKING TIME: 55–60 MIN

ingredients ※ ※ ※ ※ ※ ※ ※ ※ ※ ※

½ cup (80 g) fresh cranberries
½ cup (85 g) chocolate chips
3 cups (360 g) all-purpose flour
1 teaspoon cinnamon
1½ teaspoon baking powder
½ teaspoon salt
1⅛ cups (270 g) unsalted butter, softened (2¼ sticks)
1½ cups (300 g) sugar
2 teaspoons orange zest
5 large eggs, room temperature
1 cup (240 ml) milk, warmed
½ cup (120 ml) orange juice
2 tablespoons honey
Marzipan leaves and berries, for garnish
Confectioners' sugar, for dusting

method ※ ※ ※ ※ ※ ※ ※ ※ ※ ※

1. Preheat oven to 325°F (170°C). Spray Bundt pan with baking spray or grease and dust lightly with flour, tapping out any excess.

2. Chop cranberries coarsely and mix with chocolate chips and set aside.

3. In a large bowl, sift flour, cinnamon, baking powder and salt together. Set aside.

4. Using an electric mixer on medium speed, beat butter, sugar and orange zest until smooth and creamy, about 4 minutes. Beat in 1 egg at a time. Scrape sides of the bowl after each addition.

5. Reduce mixer speed to low. Add flour mixture in thirds, alternating with the milk and ending with flour mixture. Beat for about 30 seconds until batter is smooth.

6. Pour a third of the batter into the Bundt pan. Sprinkle with half the cranberry mixture. Pour in another third of the batter and sprinkle with remaining cranberry mixture. Pour in the remaining batter.

7. Bake the cake for 55 to 60 minutes, until a cake tester inserted near the center comes out clean. Cool in the pan for 15 minutes on a wire rack. Invert onto rack and cool completely.

8. In a saucepan, bring orange juice and honey to a boil and brush onto the cake. Let cake cool completely before serving. Garnish with fondant or marzipan holly leaves and berries. Dust lightly with confectioners' sugar to serve.

[BAKED IN THE NORDIC WARE HOLIDAY WREATH PAN]

Dark Chocolate Raspberry Cake

❄ 12 SERVINGS

PREP TIME: 35 MIN
BAKING TIME: 40–45 MIN

ingredients ❄ ❄ ❄ ❄ ❄ ❄ ❄ ❄ ❄ ❄

for cake

6 ounces (180 g) unsweetened chocolate

6 ounces (180 g) semisweet chocolate

7 large eggs, separated

1 cup (240 g) unsalted butter (2 sticks)

2 cups (400 g) sugar, divided

1½ teaspoons vanilla extract

3 tablespoons seedless raspberry preserves

1 cup (120 g) all-purpose flour

¼ cup (25 g) finely ground almonds

Fresh mint leaves, for garnish

for frosting and filling

¾ cup (180 ml) heavy cream

6 ounces (180 g) semisweet chocolate, chopped

6 ounces (170 g) frozen raspberries, thawed
   and drained

¼ cup (80 g) seedless raspberry preserves

method ❄ ❄ ❄ ❄ ❄ ❄ ❄ ❄ ❄ ❄

for cake

1. Preheat oven to 300°F (150°C). Line the bottoms
of 2 round 9-inch (23 cm) cake pans with parchment
paper. Grease the sides of the pans.

2. Melt the unsweetened and semisweet chocolate
together in the top of a double boiler. Let cool
5 minutes and beat in the egg yolks.

3. In a large bowl, using an electric mixer on
medium-high speed, beat butter, 1½ cups (300 g)
sugar and vanilla until light and fluffy. Reduce speed
to low, add the chocolate mixture and raspberry
preserves and beat until blended and smooth. Stir
in flour and almonds until just combined.

4. In a separate bowl, using an electric mixer on high
speed, beat egg whites until light and foamy. Slowly
add the remaining ½ cup (100 g) sugar. Beat until
soft peaks form. In 3 additions, fold egg whites into
chocolate batter. Pour batter into prepared pans
and gently smooth tops.

5. Bake for 40 to 45 minutes, until a cake tester
inserted into the centers comes out with a few
moist crumbs attached. Cool in the pans for
5 minutes on a wire rack. Remove from pans and
cool completely.

for frosting and filling

1. In a saucepan over medium-high heat, bring cream
to a boil. Stir the chopped chocolate into the
cream. Remove from heat and continue stirring until
chocolate has melted and mixture is smooth.

2. Pour frosting into a bowl, let cool and cover
with plastic wrap pressed against the chocolate.
Refrigerate until thick enough to spread.

3. Combine the thawed, drained raspberries and
preserves. Spread the raspberry filling between the
cake layers. Generously spoon and drizzle chocolate
frosting over the cake. Serve.

Chocolate Vanilla Village

❄ 4 SERVINGS

PREP TIME: 20 MIN
BAKING TIME: 35–40 MIN

ingredients ❊ ❊ ❊ ❊ ❊ ❊ ❊ ❊ ❊

for cake

1¾ cups (210 g) all-purpose flour

1 teaspoon baking powder

½ teaspoon salt

10 tablespoons (150 g) unsalted butter, softened
    (1¼ sticks)

½ cup (100 g) sugar

2 large eggs, room temperature

1 teaspoon vanilla extract

¾ cup (180 ml) milk, warmed

3 ounces (90 g) semisweet chocolate, chopped

to decorate

¾ cup (90 g) confectioners' sugar

1 tablespoon lemon juice

Food coloring

Decorative sugar crystals

method ❊ ❊ ❊ ❊ ❊ ❊ ❊ ❊ ❊

for cake

1. Preheat the oven to 325°F (170°C). Spray Bundt pan with baking spray or grease and dust lightly with flour, tapping out any excess.

2. In a bowl sift flour, baking powder and salt together. Set aside.

3. Using an electric mixer on medium speed, beat butter and sugar until smooth and creamy, about 4 minutes. Beat in 1 egg at a time. Scrape sides of the bowl after each addition. Add vanilla.

4. Gradually stir in flour mixture and milk. Divide the batter into 2 bowls.

5. Melt chocolate in a microwave safe bowl on medium for 1 to 2 minutes. Stir into half of the batter. Pour the light batter into the Bundt pan, followed by the dark batter.

6. Bake for 35 to 40 minutes. Cool in the pan for 10 minutes on a wire rack. Invert onto rack and cool completely.

to decorate

1. In a small bowl, combine confectioners' sugar and lemon juice, stirring until smooth.

2. If using more than 1 color, divide icing into separate bowls. Add food coloring. Using a small paintbrush, decorate the houses with the icing.

[BAKED IN THE NORDIC WARE COZY VILLAGE PAN]

Layered Gateau with Berries

❄ 8 SERVINGS

PREP TIME: 40 MIN
BAKING TIME: 15–20 MIN

ingredients ❄ ❄ ❄ ❄ ❄ ❄ ❄ ❄ ❄ ❄

for cake

6 large eggs, separated
1 cup (200 g) sugar, divided
1⅓ cups (180 g) cake flour, sifted
2 teaspoons baking powder
⅓ cup (80 ml) cold water
1 teaspoon vanilla extract

for fruit filling

1 cup (240 g) unsalted butter (2 sticks)
¼ cup (60 ml) heavy cream
1½ cups (140 g) sliced almonds
1 cup (200 g) sugar
2½ pounds (1 kg) fresh mixed berries

Confectioners' sugar, for dusting
Fresh mint

method ❄ ❄ ❄ ❄ ❄ ❄ ❄ ❄ ❄ ❄

for cake

1. Preheat oven to 350°F (180°C). Lightly grease and flour 2 round 8-inch (20 cm) cake pans.

2. Place egg yolks in a large bowl and beat well. Gradually add ¾ cup (150 g) sugar. Add flour and baking powder, alternating with water. Mix well and add vanilla.

3. In a separate bowl, beat egg whites until foamy. Slowly add remaining sugar and beat until soft peaks form. Gently fold egg whites into cake batter. Pour batter into prepared pans and bake for 15 to 20 minutes, until a cake tester inserted into the center comes out clean. Cool in the pans for 10 minutes on a wire rack. Invert onto wire rack and cool completely.

for fruit filling

1. In a saucepan over medium heat, combine the butter and cream. Stir until the butter is melted. Add the almonds and sugar, stirring frequently until caramelized and thickened. Let cool.

2. Wash and dry the berries. Slice any large pieces of fruit. Reserve a few whole berries for garnish.

to assemble

1. Carefully cut each cake horizontally into 3 layers. Spread each with a thin layer of almond cream and top with a layer of berries. Repeat, stacking all the layers.

2. Garnish with reserved whole berries, confectioners' sugar and mint. Refrigerate until ready to serve.

Cherry Cream-Filled Sponge Cake Roll

✳ 6–8 SERVINGS

PREP TIME: 3 HR 40 MIN
BAKING TIME: 8–10 MIN
CHILLING TIME: 3 HR

ingredients ✳ ✳ ✳ ✳ ✳ ✳ ✳ ✳ ✳ ✳

for cake

4 large eggs, room temperature

1 egg yolk

⅓ cup (45 g) cake flour, sifted, plus extra

3 tablespoons cornstarch

½ cup (100 g) sugar, plus 1 tablespoon

1 teaspoon vanilla extract

¼ teaspoon cream of tartar

Confectioners' sugar, for dusting

for cherry whipped cream

1 cup (240 ml) heavy cream

2 tablespoons sugar

½ teaspoon vanilla extract

¼ cup (80 g) cherry jelly or jam

1 cup (180 g) canned pitted black cherries, drained

method ✳ ✳ ✳ ✳ ✳ ✳ ✳ ✳ ✳ ✳

for cake

1. Separate 2 of the eggs, placing the yolks in a large bowl and the whites in another bowl. Add the 2 remaining eggs and the yolk to the bowl with the yolks. Set aside at room temperature.

2. Position the oven rack in the center of the oven. Preheat oven to 400°F (200°C). Line a rimmed 12 x 17-inch (30 x 45 cm) jellyroll pan with parchment paper. Coat the parchment paper with baking spray or grease and dust lightly with flour, tapping out any excess.

3. In a small bowl, whisk flour and cornstarch together. Set aside.

4. Add ½ cup (100 g) sugar to the bowl with the egg yolks. With an electric mixer on high speed, beat until mixture is pale yellow and thick, about 5 minutes. Beat in the vanilla.

5. Sift half of the flour mixture over the egg mixture and fold gently using a rubber spatula until flour is just blended. Sift the remaining flour into the batter and fold in gently.

6. In a separate bowl, beat the egg whites until foamy. Add the cream of tartar and beat until soft peaks form. Slowly add 1 tablespoon of sugar and beat until stiff peaks form. Gently fold the egg whites into the batter in 3 additions.

7. Pour the batter into the prepared pan, spreading evenly. Bake until light golden brown for 8 to 10 minutes or until the center of the cake springs back when lightly touched.

8. Dust a clean kitchen towel with confectioners' sugar. Invert cake onto the kitchen towel. Gently remove the parchment paper. Starting at the short end, roll cake in the towel. Cool completely on a wire rack, seam side down.

for cherry whipped cream

Place the cream, sugar and vanilla into a chilled bowl and beat until soft peaks form. Add the jelly and continue beating until stiff peaks form. Gently fold in the well-drained cherries.

to assemble

Unroll the sponge cake from the towel, spread the cream mixture evenly over the top and reroll, ensuring towel is only on exterior of cake. Cover and refrigerate for at least 3 hours. Just before serving, dust with confectioners' sugar.

Holiday Honey Torte

❄ 8 SERVINGS

PREP TIME: 1 HR
BAKING TIME: 5 MIN

ingredients ✳ ✳ ✳ ✳ ✳ ✳ ✳ ✳ ✳ ✳ ✳

for torte

3 large eggs
2 cups (400 g) sugar
¾ cup (180 g) unsalted butter (1½ sticks)
6 tablespoons (125 g) honey
1½ teaspoons baking soda
½ teaspoon salt
5 cups (600 g) all-purpose flour, sifted, divided

for filling

16 ounces (450 g) sour cream
2 cups (400 g) sugar
2 tablespoons honey

Happy Holidays!

method ✳ ✳ ✳ ✳ ✳ ✳ ✳ ✳ ✳ ✳

for torte

1. Preheat oven to 375°F (190°C).

2. Beat eggs together with sugar and set aside.

3. In a double boiler, melt butter and honey. Add sugar and egg mixture stirring constantly. Add baking soda and salt. Slowly stir in 4 cups (480 g) of flour, 1 cup (120 g) at a time.

4. Mound 1 cup (120 g) of flour on a clean work surface and pour the mixture into the flour. Knead the dough until smooth and pulled together. If the dough is sticky, add more flour, ¼ cup (30 g) at a time.

5. Divide the dough into 8 equal parts. Roll each piece on parchment paper, to ¹⁄₁₆-inch (.25 cm) thick. Use a round 9 to 10-inch (20 cm to 23 cm) plate to trace a circle on the rolled out dough. Cut out each circle, reserving the scraps. Place each layer on a separate parchment piece.

6. Bake 4 circles on 2 large baking sheets at a time. Add scraps to baking sheet. Bake for 5 minutes. The layers are done when they become golden. Repeat steps with remaining 4 dough circles. Layers will harden while cooling. Crumble scraps into small pieces once cake has cooled. The scraps will be used as decoration on the top and sides of the cake.

for filling

Whisk sour cream, sugar and honey together. Spread filling onto 1 cake, then continue alternating layers of cake and filling, ending with filling on top. Cake will be 8 layers tall. Let the filling run down the sides of the cake. Apply crumbles to the top and sides of the cake. Let sit for 2 hours at room temperature. Cover and refrigerate overnight.

cookies

Brownie Trees

❄ 12 TREES

PREP TIME: 25 MIN
CHILLING TIME: 1 HR
BAKING TIME: 8–11 MIN

ingredients ✳ ✳ ✳ ✳ ✳ ✳ ✳ ✳ ✳ ✳

for brownies

3 cups (360 g) all-purpose flour
½ teaspoon baking powder
½ teaspoon salt
1 cup (240 g) unsalted butter, softened
　 (2 sticks)
1½ cups (300 g) sugar
2 large eggs
1½ teaspoons vanilla extract
⅔ cup (60 g) unsweetened cocoa powder
1 teaspoon instant espresso powder

for filling

1⅓ cups (160 g) confectioners' sugar,
　 plus extra
2 tablespoons unsweetened cocoa powder
¼ cup (60 g) unsalted butter, softened
　 (½ stick)
3–4 tablespoons strong coffee (espresso
　 works well)
½ teaspoon vanilla extract

method ✳ ✳ ✳ ✳ ✳ ✳ ✳ ✳ ✳ ✳

for brownies

1. In a large bowl whisk flour, baking powder and salt together. Set aside.

2. Using an electric mixer on medium speed, cream butter and sugar together. Mix in 1 egg at a time, scraping sides of the bowl as needed. Reduce speed to low, add vanilla, cocoa and espresso powder. Mix to combine. Gradually add flour mixture, mix until smooth. Wrap dough in plastic wrap and refrigerate for at least 1 hour.

3. Preheat oven to 350°F (180°C). Line baking sheets with parchment paper.

4. On a lightly floured work surface, roll out dough to ½-inch (1 cm) thick. Using graduated star cookie cutters cut out shapes and place on prepared baking sheets.

5. Bake for 8 to 11 minutes, until just the edges are firm. Place on a wire rack to cool completely.

for filling

1. Using an electric mixer on medium speed, beat confectioners' sugar, cocoa and butter together.

2. Add coffee 1 tablespoon at a time and beat until smooth and thick. Add vanilla.

3. Use a small amount of filling between the stars to stack 3 high. Dust with confectioners' sugar to serve.

tip: Yield varies depending on the cookie cutter size.

White Chocolate Clusters

❄ 48 CLUSTERS

PREP TIME: 35 MIN
MICROWAVE TIME: 5 MIN

ingredients ✳ ✳ ✳ ✳ ✳ ✳ ✳ ✳ ✳ ✳

5 cups (140 g) corn flakes cereal
1½ cups (220 g) peanuts
1 cup (145 g) golden raisins
3 cups (500 g) white chocolate, chopped

method ✳ ✳ ✳ ✳ ✳ ✳ ✳ ✳ ✳ ✳

1. Line 2 or 3 baking sheets with parchment paper.

2. In a large bowl, combine cereal, peanuts and raisins. Set aside.

3. In a microwave safe bowl, melt the white chocolate at 70% power for 1 minute. Stir until smooth. Microwave for additional 10 to 20 second intervals, if needed.

4. Pour melted chocolate over cereal mixture. Gently stir until well coated. Working quickly, drop by spoonfuls onto prepared baking sheets.

5. Let harden until set, about 30 minutes. Store in an airtight container.

Soft and Chewy Sugar Cookies

❄ 36 COOKIES

PREP TIME: 30 MIN
CHILLING TIME: 1 HR
BAKING TIME: 6−8 MIN

ingredients ❄ ❄ ❄ ❄ ❄ ❄ ❄ ❄ ❄ ❄

¾ cup (155 g) vegetable shortening

¼ cup (60 g) unsalted butter, softened (½ stick)

1 cup (100 g) sugar

2 large eggs

½ teaspoon almond extract

½ teaspoon vanilla extract

2½ cups (300 g) all-purpose flour, plus extra
   for dusting

1 teaspoon baking powder

½ teaspoon salt

for icing

2½ tablespoons heavy cream

¼ cup (60 g) unsalted butter (½ stick)

1 teaspoon vanilla extract

2 cups (240 g) confectioners' sugar

method ❄ ❄ ❄ ❄ ❄ ❄ ❄ ❄ ❄ ❄

1. In a large bowl, beat shortening, butter, sugar,
eggs, almond and vanilla extracts with an electric
mixer on medium speed. In a separate bowl, whisk
together flour, baking powder and salt. Stir dry
mix into shortening mixture until well blended.
Refrigerate dough for at least 1 hour.

2. Preheat oven to 350°F (180°C).

3. Divide dough in half. Roll to ¼-inch (.5 cm)
thickness on a floured work surface. Cut into shapes
with cookie cutters. Place on an ungreased baking
sheet. Bake 6 to 8 minutes, until lightly golden
brown around the edges. Place cookies on a wire
rack to cool completely before decorating.

for icing

1. Heat cream and butter in a saucepan over
medium heat, until butter melts. Stir in vanilla and
confectioners' sugar.

2. Remove from heat. Beat using an electric mixer
until thick, creamy and smooth.

3. Spoon icing into a pastry bag with a very small
tip. Pipe snowflake designs on cookies. Let icing set
before serving.

tip: Yield varies based on the size of cookie cutters.

Crisp and Delicate Sugar Cookies

✳ 60 COOKIES

PREP TIME: 45 MIN
CHILLING TIME: 1 HR
BAKING TIME: 6–8 MIN

ingredients ✳ ✳ ✳ ✳ ✳ ✳ ✳ ✳ ✳ ✳

1½ cups (360 g) unsalted butter, softened (3 sticks)
2 cups (400 g) sugar
4 large eggs
1 teaspoon vanilla extract
5 cups (600 g) all-purpose flour
2 teaspoons baking powder
1 teaspoon salt

for frosting

5 cups (600 g) confectioners' sugar
½ cup (120 g) vegetable shortening
2 tablespoons unsalted butter, softened
⅓ cup (80 ml) milk
1½ teaspoons vanilla extract
Food coloring

Sugar crystals
Dragées

method ✳ ✳ ✳ ✳ ✳ ✳ ✳ ✳ ✳ ✳

1. In a large bowl, cream together butter and sugar until light, fluffy and smooth. Beat in eggs 1 at a time and vanilla. Stir in flour, baking powder and salt and stir until well blended.

2. Cover and refrigerate dough for at least 1 hour or overnight.

3. Preheat oven to 375°F (190°C).

4. Divide dough. On a lightly floured surface, roll out dough to ¼-inch (.5 cm) thick. Cut out shapes with cookie cutters. Reroll any dough scraps for more cookies.

5. Place cookies 1 inch (2.5 cm) apart on an ungreased baking sheet. Bake for 6 to 8 minutes, until lightly browned. Place on a wire rack to cool completely before decorating.

for frosting

1. In a large bowl, cream together confectioners' sugar, shortening and butter until smooth.

2. Using an electric mixer on low speed, slowly add the milk and vanilla, mixing until smooth and stiff, about 5 minutes. Add food coloring.

3. If using more than 1 color, divide the frosting into separate bowls. Frost cooled cookies and decorate with sugar crystals and dragées. Serve.

Holiday Mouse Cookies

❄ 24 COOKIES

PREP TIME: 20 MIN
CHILLING TIME: 1 HR 30 MIN

ingredients ❊ ❊ ❊ ❊ ❊ ❊ ❊ ❊ ❊ ❊

1 cup (180 g) white chocolate chips

4 teaspoons shortening, divided

24 chocolate sandwich cookies (such as Double Stuf Oreo®)

1 cup (180 g) semisweet chocolate chips

24 maraschino cherries with stems, drained, patted dry

24 milk chocolate candy kisses

48 sliced almonds

1 small tube green decorating frosting

1 small tube red decorating frosting

1 small tube white decorating frosting

1 small tube black decorating frosting

method ❊ ❊ ❊ ❊ ❊ ❊ ❊ ❊ ❊ ❊

1. In a small microwave safe bowl, melt white chocolate chips with 2 tablespoons shortening, stir until smooth.

2. Place a large piece of wax paper on a cookie sheet and dip each cookie into the white chocolate and carefully place on wax paper. Refrigerate for 1 hour.

3. In a small microwave safe bowl, melt semisweet chocolate chips with 2 tablespoons shortening, stir until smooth.

4. Remove cookies from refrigerator. Holding each cherry by the stem, dip into the semisweet chocolate. Press onto the bottom of a chocolate kiss. Place the cherry and kiss on the dipped cookie with the cherry stem extending beyond the edge of the cookie.

5. For the mouse ears, place sliced almonds between the cherry and the chocolate kiss. Refrigerate until set.

6. With green frosting, pipe a holly leaf on each cookie. With red frosting, pipe holly berries between leaves. With white frosting, place 2 small eyes on each chocolate kiss. With black frosting, place 2 small dots on top of white frosting eyes and a dot for the nose. Refrigerate until serving.

Decorated Pecan Cookies

❄ 24 COOKIES

PREP TIME: 1 HR 30 MIN
CHILLING TIME: 1 HR
BAKING TIME: 12–14 MIN

ingredients ❄ ❄ ❄ ❄ ❄ ❄ ❄ ❄ ❄ ❄

1½ cups (180 g) all-purpose flour

¼ (30 g) cup cornstarch

¼ teaspoon salt

¾ cup (180 g) unsalted butter, softened (1½ sticks)

¼ cup (50 g) sugar

¼ cup (60 g) light brown sugar, firmly packed

2 teaspoons vanilla extract

1½ cups (150 g) pecans, finely chopped

for royal icing

2 pasteurized egg whites

2 teaspoons fresh lemon juice

3 cups (360 g) confectioners' sugar, sifted

24 edible decorative holiday sugars

method ❄ ❄ ❄ ❄ ❄ ❄ ❄ ❄ ❄ ❄

1. In a bowl, whisk flour, cornstarch and salt together. Set aside.

2. Using an electric mixer on medium-high speed, beat butter, sugars and vanilla for 1 minute, until smooth and creamy.

3. Reduce speed to low, add flour mixture and pecans. Mix for 1 minute, until dough forms. Wrap dough in plastic wrap and refrigerate for at least 1 hour or up to 3 days.

4. Position oven racks in the upper and lower third of the oven. Preheat oven to 350°F (180°C). Line 2 cookie sheets with parchment paper.

5. On a lightly floured surface, roll out dough into an 11-inch (25 cm) circle, about ¼-inch (.5 cm) thick. Cut out cookies using a round 2-inch (5 cm) cookie cutter. Reroll any dough scraps for more cookies.

6. Place cookies 1 inch (2.5 cm) apart on prepared cookie sheets. Bake for 12 to 14 minutes, until the edges are golden brown. Rotate the cookie sheets half way through for even baking.

7. Cool 10 minutes on cookie sheets. Place on a wire rack to cool completely before decorating.

for royal icing

1. In a large bowl, beat the egg whites and lemon juice together until peaks form. Add the sifted confectioners' sugar and beat on low speed until smooth and well mixed.

2. Immediately frost each cookie and set a decorative sugar in the center. Let icing set until firm. Royal icing hardens when exposed to air. Use immediately or store in an airtight container.

3. Serve. Cookies can be stored in an airtight container at room temperature for up to 1 week.

Pistachio Butter Cookies with Chocolate Hazelnut Filling

❄ 30 COOKIES

PREP TIME: 35 MIN
CHILLING TIME: 1 HR
BAKING TIME: 15–18 MIN

ingredients ❄ ❄ ❄ ❄ ❄ ❄ ❄ ❄ ❄

1 cup (240 g) unsalted butter, softened (2 sticks)

¼ cup (50 g) sugar

1 large egg

½ teaspoon almond extract

2½ cups (300 g) all-purpose flour, sifted

¾ cup (95 g) pistachios, finely chopped

1 13-ounce jar (370 g) chocolate hazelnut spread, (such as Nutella)

Confectioners' sugar

method ❄ ❄ ❄ ❄ ❄ ❄ ❄ ❄ ❄

1. In a large bowl, using an electric mixer on medium speed, beat butter and sugar until light and fluffy. Scrape down the sides of the bowl. Add egg and almond extract, beating to combine. Reduce mixer speed to low, add flour and mix until combined. Add finely chopped pistachios and stir into batter.

2. Place dough on a clean work surface. Divide in half. Roll each piece into a log about 1½ inches (3.5 cm) in diameter. Wrap in plastic wrap and refrigerate until firm, about 1 hour or overnight.

3. Position oven racks in the upper and lower third of the oven. Preheat oven to 350°F (180°C). Line baking sheets with parchment paper.

4. Slice logs into rounds ¼-inch (.5 cm) thick. Place 1 inch (2.5 cm) apart on prepared baking sheets. Bake 15 to 18 minutes, until edges are golden brown. Rotate baking sheets for even baking. Place cookies on a wire rack to cool.

5. When cookies have completely cooled, spread about 1 teaspoonful of chocolate hazelnut spread on the bottom side on a cookie and top with another cookie, creating a sandwich. Repeat until all cookies have been assembled.

6. Dust cookies with confectioners' sugar. Serve.

Bear Paw Cookies

❄ 36 COOKIES

PREP TIME: 25 MIN
BAKING TIME: 15–20 MIN

ingredients ❅ ❅ ❅ ❅ ❅ ❅ ❅ ❅ ❅ ❅

¾ cup (110 g) almonds

1 cup + 5 tablespoons (400 g) unsalted butter, softened (2⅔ sticks)

2¼ cups (450 g) sugar, plus extra

2 large eggs

3 cups (360 g) all-purpose flour

1 teaspoon cinnamon

½ teaspoon ground cloves

½ cup (45 g) unsweetened cocoa powder

method ❅ ❅ ❅ ❅ ❅ ❅ ❅ ❅ ❅ ❅

1. Preheat oven to 350°F (180°C). Coat 3 bear paw molds or madeleine pans thoroughly with baking spray. Work in batches, if needed, cooling pans between baking.

2. In a food processor, grind almonds until a crumbly paste forms. Set aside.

3. In a large bowl, cream together butter and sugar. Add 1 egg at a time and mix well.

4. In a separate bowl, whisk together flour, cinnamon, cloves, cocoa powder and ground almonds. Add dry ingredients to the butter mixture. Mix well.

5. Press dough into the prepared pans and bake for 15 to 20 minutes, until a cake tester inserted in the center of a cookie comes out clean. Cool cookies in the pan for 5 minutes on a wire rack before gently sliding them out of the pans.

6. Cool completely and sprinkle with sugar. Serve.

Peanut Blossoms

❄ 48 COOKIES

PREP TIME: 20 MIN
BAKING TIME: 8–10 MIN

ingredients ❄ ❄ ❄ ❄ ❄ ❄ ❄ ❄ ❄ ❄

1 bag milk chocolate candy kisses
1¾ cups (210 g) all-purpose flour
1 teaspoon baking soda
½ teaspoon salt
½ cup (120 g) unsalted butter, softened (1 stick)
½ cup (130 g) creamy peanut butter
½ cup (100 g) sugar, plus extra
½ cup 100 g) brown sugar, firmly packed
1 large egg
1 tablespoon milk

method ❄ ❄ ❄ ❄ ❄ ❄ ❄ ❄ ❄ ❄

1. Preheat oven to 375°F (190°C). Remove the foil wrap from approximately 48 candy kisses.

2. Sift flour, baking soda and salt together. In a large mixing bowl, cream butter and peanut butter, beat until fluffy. Add sugars, egg and milk and mix well. Add dry ingredients and mix well.

3. Shape dough into 1-inch (2.5 cm) balls using a teaspoon. Roll in sugar to coat. Place on ungreased cookie sheets.

4. Bake for 8 to 10 minutes, until lightly browned. Remove from oven and gently press a candy kiss into each cookie. Cookies will crack around the edges. Return to oven and bake for 30 to 60 seconds longer, taking care not to burn the chocolate.

5. Remove from cookie sheets to wire rack. Cool completely. Store in an airtight container.

Chocolate Turtle Cookies

❄ 24 COOKIES

PREP TIME: 20 MIN
CHILLING TIME: 1 HR
BAKING TIME: 12 MIN

ingredients ❈ ❈ ❈ ❈ ❈ ❈ ❈ ❈ ❈ ❈

1 cup (120 g) all-purpose flour
⅓ cup (30 g) unsweetened cocoa powder
½ teaspoon salt
½ cup (120 g) unsalted butter, softened (1 stick)
⅔ cup (130 g) sugar
1 large egg, separated
2 tablespoons milk
1 teaspoon vanilla extract
1 egg white
1¼ cups (140 g) pecans, finely chopped
14 soft caramel candies
3 tablespoons heavy cream

method ❈ ❈ ❈ ❈ ❈ ❈ ❈ ❈ ❈ ❈

1. In a medium bowl, whisk flour, cocoa powder and salt together. Using an electric mixer on medium-high speed, beat butter and sugar together until light and fluffy, about 2 to 3 minutes. Add the egg yolk, milk and vanilla. Mix well. Reduce mixer speed to low and gradually beat in the flour until just combined.

2. Place dough on a clean work surface, shape into a ball and flatten into a disk. Wrap in plastic wrap and refrigerate for about 1 hour or until firm.

3. Position oven racks in the upper and lower third of the oven. Preheat oven to 350°F (180°C). Line 2 baking sheets with parchment paper.

4. In a small bowl, whisk the 2 egg whites until foamy. Place the chopped pecans in a shallow bowl.

5. Remove firm dough from the refrigerator. Break off 1-inch (2.5 cm) pieces and roll into balls. Roll the balls in the egg whites, coating completely. Then roll in the pecans. Place on prepared baking sheets about 2 inches (5 cm) apart. Using a small teaspoon, make an indentation in the center of each ball.

6. Bake cookies for about 12 minutes or until set. Rotate the baking sheets half way through for even baking. When done, remove from oven and repeat the indentation in the center of each cookie. Let cool for 5 minutes on the baking sheets. Place cookies on a wire rack to cool completely.

7. Place caramels and heavy cream in a microwave safe bowl. Heat for 30 seconds and stir. Heat again, until caramels are smooth and completely melted. Allow caramel to cool slightly. Fill each cookie with ½ teaspoon caramel mixture. Cool completely before serving.

Hazelnut Brownies with White Chocolate Frosting

❄ 24 BROWNIES

PREP TIME: 30 MIN
COOKING TIME: 30 MIN

ingredients ❄ ❄ ❄ ❄ ❄ ❄ ❄ ❄ ❄ ❄

2½ cups (425 g) semisweet chocolate chips
1 cup (240 g) unsalted butter (2 sticks)
1 cup (200 g) sugar
4 large eggs
¼ teaspoon salt
2 teaspoons vanilla extract
¾ cup (90 g) all-purpose flour
2 cups (280 g) toasted hazelnuts, divided
12 ounces (360 g) white chocolate, chopped
24 whole hazelnuts

method ❄ ❄ ❄ ❄ ❄ ❄ ❄ ❄ ❄ ❄

1. Preheat oven to 350°F (180°C). Butter and flour a 9 x 13-inch (23 x 32 cm) pan.

2. Stir chocolate chips and butter in heavy saucepan over medium-low heat until melted and smooth. Remove from heat.

3. Combine sugar, eggs and salt in heavy large saucepan. Whisk constantly over low heat until sugar dissolves, about 4 minutes. Remove from heat. Whisk in chocolate mixture and vanilla.

4. Stir in flour and 1 cup (140 g) of coarsely chopped hazelnuts. Spread batter in prepared pan. Bake for about 30 minutes, until a cake tester inserted into the center comes out with a few moist crumbs attached. Cool brownies completely in the pan on a wire rack. Cut into 2-inch (5 cm) squares.

5. Place remaining chopped hazelnuts in a shallow bowl.

6. Stir white chocolate in the top of a double boiler over barely simmering water until smooth. Remove from heat. Dip sides of the cooled brownies in the melted chocolate and then dip each side in the chopped nuts.

7. Place dipped brownies on a serving plate and spread remaining white chocolate over the tops. Place 1 whole hazelnut on each brownie. Serve.

Pecan Triangles

❄ 48 COOKIES

PREP TIME: 15 MIN
BAKING TIME: 37–45 MIN

ingredients ✳ ✳ ✳ ✳ ✳ ✳ ✳ ✳ ✳ ✳

for crust

½ cup (240 g) unsalted butter, softened (1 stick)
½ cup (100 g) brown sugar, packed
1 egg yolk
1½ cups (180 g) all-purpose flour

for topping

1 cup (200 g) brown sugar, packed
½ cup (240 g) unsalted butter (1 stick)
¼ cup (60 ml) honey
½ cup (120 ml) heavy cream
4 cups (400 g) pecans, chopped

method ✳ ✳ ✳ ✳ ✳ ✳ ✳ ✳ ✳ ✳

for crust

1. Preheat oven to 350°F (180°C). Line a 9 x 13-inch (23 x 32 cm) baking pan with parchment paper, overlapping the sides of the pan with parchment. Butter the parchment with about 2 teaspoons of butter. Set aside.

2. In a large bowl, using an electric mixer on medium speed, cream butter and brown sugar together until light and fluffy. Beat in egg yolk. Slowly add flour and mix well.

3. Press dough into the prepared baking pan. Bake for 12 to 15 minutes, until golden brown.

for topping

1. In a large saucepan, stir the brown sugar, butter and honey together. Bring to a boil over medium heat. Stir constantly for 3 minutes. Remove from heat, stir in cream and pecans. Pour pecan mixture over the crust. Bake for 25 to 30 minutes, until bubbly. Cool in the pan on a wire rack.

2. Use the overlapping parchment to lift the cookies out of the pan and place on a cutting board. Cut into 24 bars and then cut each bar in half diagonally for triangles. Serve.

Chocolate Pinwheel Cookies

❄ 48 COOKIES

PREP TIME: 40 MIN
CHILLING TIME: 2 HR 10 MIN
BAKING TIME: 10–12 MIN

ingredients ❄ ❄ ❄ ❄ ❄ ❄ ❄ ❄ ❄ ❄

2½ cups (300 g) all-purpose flour

¼ teaspoon baking soda

¼ teaspoon salt

1 cup (240 g) unsalted butter, softened (2 sticks)

¾ cup (150 g) sugar

1 large egg

1 teaspoon vanilla extract

¼ cup (30 g) confectioners' sugar

4 ounces (120 g) semisweet chocolate, melted

2 tablespoons unsweetened cocoa powder

method ❄ ❄ ❄ ❄ ❄ ❄ ❄ ❄ ❄ ❄

1. In a medium bowl, whisk together flour, baking soda and salt. Set aside.

2. In a large bowl, using an electric mixer on medium speed, cream the butter and sugar together for 1 minute. Scrape the sides of the bowl as needed. Add the egg and vanilla and beat until well mixed. Reduce mixer speed to low, gradually beat in flour mixture until just blended.

3. Divide dough in half. In 1 bowl, add confectioners' sugar, melted chocolate and cocoa powder and stir until well blended.

4. On a sheet of waxed paper, roll out the chocolate dough into a 10 x 14-inch (26 x 36 cm) rectangle. Repeat with the plain dough. Place the plain dough on top of the chocolate dough. Refrigerate the dough for about 10 minutes.

5. Once firm, peel off the top sheet of waxed paper. Starting with the long side, tightly roll rectangles together, jellyroll style, to form a log. Cut log in half, crosswise. Wrap each log in plastic wrap and freeze for about 2 hours or refrigerate overnight.

6. Preheat oven to 350°F (180°C). Work with 1 log at a time. Using a sharp knife, cut into slices ¼-inch (.5 cm) thick. Place slices 2 inches (5 cm) apart on an ungreased cookie sheet. Bake for 10 to 12 minutes or until lightly browned. Place cookies on a wire rack to cool completely. Repeat with remaining chilled log. Serve.

Almond Meringues with Chocolate Drizzle

✻ 20 COOKIES

PREP TIME: 25 MIN
BAKING TIME: 2–3 HR

ingredients ✻ ✻ ✻ ✻ ✻ ✻ ✻ ✻ ✻ ✻

4 egg whites
½ teaspoon cream of tartar
1 cup (200 g) superfine sugar, divided
1 teaspoon vanilla extract
1¼ cups (125 g) ground almonds
4 ounces (120 g) semisweet chocolate, chopped

method ✻ ✻ ✻ ✻ ✻ ✻ ✻ ✻ ✻ ✻

1. Preheat oven to 350°F (180°C). Line 2 baking sheets with parchment paper.

2. In the bowl of an electric mixer, beat egg whites until foamy. Add cream of tartar and beat until fluffy peaks form. Add ½ cup (100 g) of the sugar gradually. Add vanilla. Add the remaining ½ cup (100 g) of the sugar very slowly, until the meringue is shiny and the sugar is completely dissolved. Gently fold in the ground almonds, taking care not to overmix.

3. Immediately spoon the meringue into a pastry bag fitted with a large tip. Pipe circles about 2 inches (5 cm) in diameter on the baking sheets, leaving 1 inch (2.5 cm) between each meringue.

4. Place baking sheets in the oven and turn the oven off. Leave cookies in the oven undisturbed for at least 2 or 3 hours or even overnight, until cookies are dry and crisp.

5. In a microwave safe bowl, melt the chopped chocolate on high for 1 minute. Stir. Microwave for additional 30 second intervals as needed. Stir until chocolate is completely melted.

6. With cookies still on parchment paper, drizzle with melted chocolate using a fork. Allow chocolate to set. Serve.

Cranberry White Chocolate Macadamia Cookies

❄ 36 COOKIES

PREP TIME: 20 MIN
BAKING TIME: 16–18 MIN

ingredients ❄ ❄ ❄ ❄ ❄ ❄ ❄ ❄ ❄ ❄

3 cups (360 g) all-purpose flour

½ teaspoon salt

1 teaspoon baking soda

1 cup (240 g) unsalted butter, softened (2 sticks)

1 cup (220 g) light brown sugar, packed

¾ cup (150 g) sugar

2 large eggs

1 tablespoon vanilla extract

1 cup (120 g) dried cranberries

1½ cups (250 g) white chocolate chips

1 cup (140 g) macadamia nuts, chopped

method ❄ ❄ ❄ ❄ ❄ ❄ ❄ ❄ ❄ ❄

1. Preheat oven to 350°F (180°C). Line 2 baking sheets with parchment paper.

2. Sift flour, salt and baking soda into a medium bowl. Set aside. In a large bowl, using an electric mixer on medium-high speed, beat butter until light and fluffy. Add the sugars and beat until blended. Beat in 1 egg at a time. Add vanilla.

3. Add dry ingredients and beat until just mixed. Using a spatula, fold in the cranberries, white chocolate chips and chopped nuts.

4. For large cookies, drop dough by heaping tablespoonfuls onto prepared baking sheets, spacing about 2½ inches (6 cm) apart. For smaller cookies, drop by heaping teaspoonfuls, spacing 1½ inches (3.5 cm) apart.

5. Bake cookies until just golden, about 16 to 18 minutes for large cookies and about 14 to 15 minutes for small cookies. Cool on baking sheets for 5 minutes and place on a wire rack to cool completely. Serve.

holiday specialties

Rum Truffles

❄ 36 TRUFFLES

PREP TIME: 10 MIN
BAKING TIME: 8 MIN
CHILLING TIME: 1 HR

ingredients ❄ ❄ ❄ ❄ ❄ ❄ ❄ ❄ ❄ ❄ ❄

1½ cups (150 g) pecans
1¼ cups (140 g) chocolate wafer cookies crumbs
½ cup (60 g) confectioners' sugar
2 tablespoons unsweetened cocoa powder
3 tablespoons light corn syrup
¼ cup (60 ml) rum

optional decoration

4 ounces (110 g) marzipan paste
3 tablespoons confectioners' sugar, plus extra
Red and green food coloring

method ❄ ❄ ❄ ❄ ❄ ❄ ❄ ❄ ❄ ❄

1. Position oven rack in the center of the oven and preheat to 350°F (180°C). Place the pecans on a baking sheet and bake for about 8 minutes, until fragrant and lightly browned. Cool completely. Place in a food processor and pulse until finely chopped. Transfer to a large bowl.

2. Process the chocolate wafers in the food processor until finely ground and add to the pecans. Add confectioners' sugar and cocoa powder, stirring well. Add the corn syrup and rum and mix well. Chill for at least 1 hour.

3. Shape into 1-inch (2.5 cm) balls and dust with confectioners' sugar

optional decoration

Knead the marzipan with the confectioners' sugar. Divide the marzipan in half. Color one half with red coloring and roll into small balls for the berries. Color the remaining half with green coloring and shape into holly leaves. Dust with confectioners' sugar and add the marzipan leaves and berries. Serve.

Chocolate Peppermint Candies

❄ 32 CANDIES

PREP TIME: 10 MIN
MICROWAVE TIME: 2 MIN
CHILLING TIME: 40 MIN

ingredients ❄ ❄ ❄ ❄ ❄ ❄ ❄ ❄ ❄ ❄

1 can sweetened condensed milk

1 tablespoon peppermint extract

4½–5 cups (450–500 g) confectioners' sugar, sifted, divided

3 cups (510 g) semisweet chocolate chips

3 tablespoons vegetable shortening

method ❄ ❄ ❄ ❄ ❄ ❄ ❄ ❄ ❄ ❄

1. Fold a 24-inch (60 cm) sheet of parchment paper accordion-style so that it has 8 folds, each 3 inches (7.5 cm) wide. Trace a 3-inch (7.5 cm) circle 4 times onto the folded parchment, then cut circles fully. You should end up with 32 parchment circles. Spread out onto a baking sheet so that none of the circles overlap.

2. Combine condensed milk, peppermint extract and 2 cups (200 g) of confectioners' sugar in a large mixing bowl. Using an electric mixer on medium speed, beat until well blended. Add more confectioners' sugar, ½ cup (50 g) at a time, until dough is stiff and not sticky.

3. Roll the dough into 1-inch (2.5 cm) balls. Place 1 on each parchment circle. Flatten dough to form patties. Place in the freezer for no longer than 30 minutes.

4. In a microwave safe bowl, melt the chocolate chips for 30 seconds. Stir until smooth. Microwave for additional 10 to 20 second intervals, if needed. Stir in the shortening until smooth.

5. Remove candies from freezer. Place a candy on the tines of a fork and dip in the melted chocolate until completely covered. Allow any excess chocolate to drip back into the bowl before placing each candy back on the parchment paper circles.

6. Refrigerate until firm. Candies are ready when they are dry to the touch. Serve candies with parchment attached to avoid sticking.

Vanilla Peppermint Cupcakes

❄ 12 CUPCAKES

PREP TIME: 25 MIN
BAKING TIME: 18—20 MIN

ingredients ✳ ✳ ✳ ✳ ✳ ✳ ✳ ✳ ✳ ✳

for cupcakes

1½ cups (180 g) all-purpose flour, sifted

1 teaspoon baking powder

½ cup (120 ml) milk

1 teaspoon vanilla extract

1 teaspoon peppermint extract

½ cup (120 g) unsalted butter, softened (1 stick)

1 cup (200 g) sugar

1 large egg, room temperature

2 egg whites, room temperature

for frosting

1 cup (240 g) unsalted butter, softened (2 sticks)

3½ cups (350 g) confectioners' sugar, sifted

½ teaspoon peppermint extract

½ teaspoon vanilla extract

1 teaspoon milk, plus extra

6 red white and green candy canes, crushed

method ✳ ✳ ✳ ✳ ✳ ✳ ✳ ✳ ✳ ✳

for cupcakes

1. Preheat oven to 350°F (180°C). Line a 12-cup muffin tin with holiday foil cupcake liners.

2. In a medium bowl, sift flour and baking powder together. Set aside. In a small bowl, mix milk, vanilla and peppermint extracts together.

3. In a large bowl, using an electric mixer on medium-high speed, beat butter and sugar together until light and fluffy. Reduce mixer speed to medium and gradually add egg and egg whites. Scrape down the sides of the bowl, as needed.

4. Reduce mixer speed to low. Add flour mixture in thirds, alternating with the milk mixture and ending with flour mixture. Beat for about 30 seconds, until batter is smooth.

5. Divide batter evenly between prepared muffin tins. Bake for 18 to 20 minutes, until a cake tester inserted into the centers comes out clean. Cool completely in the pan on a wire rack before frosting.

for frosting

1. In a large bowl, using an electric mixer on medium speed beat the butter until light and fluffy, about 2 minutes.

2. Reduce mixer speed to low. Slowly add confectioners' sugar and beat until well blended. Add peppermint, vanilla extracts and milk. Continue beating until smooth and creamy. Add additional milk, 1 teaspoon at a time if needed to thin.

3. Spread frosting on each cupcake. Top with crushed candy canes. Serve.

Chocolate Bark with Cranberries and Pistachios

✳ 1 POUND (.5 KG)

PREP TIME: 14 MIN
MICROWAVE TIME: 2–5 MIN
CHILLING TIME: 1 HR

ingredients ✳ ✳ ✳ ✳ ✳ ✳ ✳ ✳ ✳ ✳

6 ounces (180 g) semisweet chocolate, chopped

6 ounces (180 g) premium white chocolate, chopped

1 cup (125 g) pistachio nuts, roasted, roughly chopped

1 cup (120 g) dried cranberries

method ✳ ✳ ✳ ✳ ✳ ✳ ✳ ✳ ✳ ✳

1. Line a baking sheet with parchment paper.

2. In a microwave safe bowl, melt the semisweet chocolate on high for 1 to 2 minutes or until almost melted, stirring once. Microwave for additional 10 to 20 second intervals, if needed. Remove and stir until completely melted.

3. In a microwave safe bowl, melt the white chocolate on high for 1 to 2 minutes or until almost melted, stirring once. Microwave for additional 10 to 20 second intervals, if needed. Remove and stir until completely melted.

4. Stir half of the pistachios and half of the cranberries into each bowl.

5. Alternating between the semisweet and white chocolates, spoon onto the prepared baking sheet. Swirl chocolates together with a knife to marbleize.

6. Refrigerate for at least 1 hour or until firm. Break into pieces. Serve.

Cinnamon Mini Muffins

✳ 12 MUFFINS

PREP TIME: 20 MIN
BAKING TIME: 20–25 MIN

ingredients ✳ ✳ ✳ ✳ ✳ ✳ ✳ ✳ ✳ ✳

1½ cups (180 g) all-purpose flour
1 teaspoon baking powder
⅛ teaspoon salt
½ cup (120 g) unsalted butter, softened (1 stick)
½ cup (100 g) sugar
1 large egg, room temperature
1 egg yolk
½ cup (120 ml) milk, warmed
1 teaspoon cinnamon
1 teaspoon unsweetened cocoa powder

for glaze

1 cup (240 ml) apple juice
1 cup (120 g) confectioners' sugar, sifted

Decorative sugar
Candy stars

method ✳ ✳ ✳ ✳ ✳ ✳ ✳ ✳ ✳ ✳

1. Position an oven rack at the lowest level and preheat oven to 375°F (190°C). Spray pan with baking spray and dust lightly with flour, tapping out any excess.

2. In a bowl, sift flour, baking powder and salt together. Set aside.

3. Using an electric mixer on medium speed, beat butter and sugar until smooth and creamy, about 4 minutes. Add egg and egg yolk and mix well.

4. Gradually stir in flour mixture and milk. Divide batter into 2 bowls. Stir cinnamon and cocoa powder into 1 bowl. Alternate pouring the 2 bowls of batter into the prepared pan and stir twice with a toothpick.

5. Bake muffins for 20 to 25 minutes. Cool in the pan for 5 minutes on a wire rack. Invert onto rack and cool completely.

for glaze

In a saucepan, reduce apple juice by three quarters. Whisk reduced apple juice and sugar together until smooth and brush onto muffins. Sprinkle with decorative sugar and and candy stars.

[BAKED IN THE NORDIC WARE MINI MUFFIN PAN]

holiday specialties

Tree-Shaped Dinner Rolls

❄ 25 ROLLS

PREP TIME: 25 MIN
RISING TIME: 2 HR
BAKING TIME: 20–25 MIN

ingredients ❋ ❋ ❋ ❋ ❋ ❋ ❋ ❋ ❋ ❋

2 packages active dry yeast
½ cup (100 g) sugar
1½ teaspoons ground cardamom
4¾ cups (570 g) all-purpose flour, plus extra, divided
1½ teaspoons salt, plus ⅛ teaspoon
½ cup (120 g) unsalted butter (1 stick)
1 cup (240 ml) water
2 large eggs, separated

to decorate

¾ cup (90 g) confectioners' sugar
1 tablespoon lemon juice
15 candied cherries
30 pistachios
Whipped butter, for serving

method ❋ ❋ ❋ ❋ ❋ ❋ ❋ ❋ ❋ ❋

1. In a large bowl, combine yeast, sugar, cardamom, 1½ cups (180 g) flour, and 1½ teaspoons salt. In a small saucepan over low heat, heat butter in water until very warm, about 125°F (50°C). Butter need not melt completely.

2. Using an electric mixer on low speed, add melted butter mixture to dry ingredients. Mix until just blended. Increase mixer speed to medium, beat 2 minutes, scraping down the sides of the bowl. Beat in 1 egg and 1 egg yolk. (Refrigerate the remaining egg white to use later.) Add ½ cup (60 g) flour and continue beating for an additional 2 minutes. Stir in 2½ cups (300 g) flour, mixing until the dough is soft and smooth.

3. On a lightly floured surface, knead dough until smooth and elastic, about 8 minutes. Work in the remaining ¼ cup (30 g) flour if needed. Shape the dough into a large ball. Place in a large greased bowl, turning to fully coat the dough. Cover with plastic wrap and let rise in a warm place until doubled in size, about 1 hour.

4. Punch dough down. Cut dough into 25 pieces. Let rest for about 15 minutes. Shape dough into 21 small balls, about walnut size. Shape the remaining dough into an oval shape to form the tree trunk. Using a sharp knife, cut a shallow slit lengthwise into the top of the tree trunk.

to assemble tree

1. Lightly grease a large baking sheet. Place 1 dough ball at the top. Make a second row by centering 2 dough balls directly under the first ball. Leave about ¼ inch (.5 cm) between balls for rising. Continue making rows, increasing each row by 1 dough ball, until there are 6 rows. Use the remaining dough for the tree trunk. Cover with a clean towel and let rise until doubled, about 45 minutes.

2. Preheat oven to 375°F (190°C). In a small bowl, beat reserved egg white and ⅛ teaspoon salt with a fork until foamy. Brush rolls with egg white. Bake rolls for 20 to 25 minutes until golden brown. Rolls should sound hollow when tapped lightly. Cool completely on a wire rack.

to decorate

In a small bowl, combine confectioners' sugar and lemon juice, stirring until smooth. Spoon glaze into a pastry bag and pipe garland into cooled rolls. Decorate with candied cherries and pistachios. Serve with whipped butter.

Peppermint Meringues

❄ 36 CANDIES

PREP TIME: 15 MIN
BAKING TIME: 2 HR

ingredients ❄ ❄ ❄ ❄ ❄ ❄ ❄ ❄ ❄

4 egg whites, room temperature
2¼ cups (300 g) confectioners' sugar
¼ teaspoon peppermint extract

method ❄ ❄ ❄ ❄ ❄ ❄ ❄ ❄ ❄

1. Preheat the oven to 200°F (100°C). Line a baking sheet with parchment paper.

2. In a mixing bowl, whip egg whites with an electric mixer until foamy. Gradually add sugar, whipping at medium speed. When stiff peaks form, add peppermint extract and whip until mixed.

3. Transfer mixture to a large pastry bag. Pipe the meringue onto the prepared baking sheet using a large star tip, 1 inch (2.5 cm) apart.

4. Place the meringues in the oven. Bake for 2 hours or until meringues are dry but not brown. Cool completely before storing in an airtight container.

Pecan Sticky Buns

❄ 12 SERVINGS

PREP TIME: 25 MIN
RISING TIME: 2 HR
BAKING TIME: 30–35 MIN

ingredients ❄ ❄ ❄ ❄ ❄ ❄ ❄ ❄ ❄ ❄

1 package active dry yeast
¾ cup (180 ml) warm water
¾ cup (180 ml) warm milk
¼ cup (50 g) sugar
3 tablespoons canola oil
2 teaspoons salt
3¾ cups (450 g) all-purpose flour, plus more
   if needed, divided

for filling

¼ cup (60 g) unsalted butter, softened (½ stick)
¼ cup (50 g) sugar
3 teaspoons cinnamon
¾ cup (165 g) brown sugar, packed
½ cup (120 ml) heavy cream
1 cup (100 g) pecans, coarsely chopped

method ❄ ❄ ❄ ❄ ❄ ❄ ❄ ❄ ❄ ❄

1. In a large bowl, dissolve yeast in warm water 110°F (45°C) and let rest for 5 minutes. Add warm milk 110°F (45°C), sugar, oil, salt and 1¼ cups (150 g) flour. Using an electric mixer on medium speed, beat for 2 to 3 minutes, until smooth. Stir in 2½ cups (300 g) flour and mix until a soft dough forms. Add up to ¼ cup (30 g) more flour if needed.

2. On a lightly floured surface, knead dough until smooth and elastic, about 6 to 8 minutes. Place in a greased bowl, turning to fully coat the dough. Cover with plastic wrap and let rise in a warm place until doubled in size, about 1 hour.

3. Punch dough down and turn onto lightly floured surface. Roll into a 9 x 13-inch (23 x 32 cm) rectangle. Spread butter to within ½ inch (1 cm) of dough edges. In a small bowl, combine sugar and cinnamon. Sprinkle sugar mixture over butter. Roll from the long side of the rectangle jellyroll style. Press edges together to seal. Cut into 12 slices.

4. In a medium bowl, combine brown sugar and cream. Grease a 9 x 13-inch (23 x 32 cm) baking pan. Pour brown sugar and cream mixture into pan. Sprinkle with pecans. Place rolls cut side down on pecans. Cover and let rise until doubled in size, about 1 hour.

5. Preheat oven to 350°F (180°C). Bake for 30 to 35 minutes or until well browned. Cool for several minutes before inverting onto a serving platter. Serve.

Glazed Orange Cupcakes with Sugared Cranberries

❄ 12 CUPCAKES

PREP TIME: 30 MIN
BAKING TIME: 18–20 MIN

ingredients ✳ ✳ ✳ ✳ ✳ ✳ ✳ ✳ ✳ ✳

for cupcakes

2 cups (280 g) cake flour, sifted
2 teaspoons baking powder
½ teaspoon salt
½ cup (120 ml) milk
¼ cup (60 ml) orange juice
½ cup (120 g) unsalted butter, softened (1 stick)
1 cup (200 g) sugar
2 large eggs, room temperature
½ teaspoon vanilla extract
1 tablespoon orange zest

for glaze

1½ cups (150 g) confectioners' sugar, sifted
3 tablespoons fresh orange juice

for sugared cranberries

1 cup (200 g) sugar
1 cup (240 ml) water
1 cup (100 g) fresh cranberries
½ cup (100 g) superfine sugar

method ✳ ✳ ✳ ✳ ✳ ✳ ✳ ✳ ✳ ✳

for cupcakes

1. Preheat oven to 375°F (190°C). Spray a 12-cup muffin pan with baking spray.

2. In a medium bowl, sift flour, baking powder and salt together. Set aside. In a small bowl, combine milk with orange juice.

3. Using an electric mixer on medium speed, beat butter and sugar together until light and fluffy. Beat in 1 egg at a time. Scrape sides of the bowl and add vanilla and orange zest.

4. Reduce mixer speed to low. Add flour mixture in thirds, alternating with the milk mixture and ending with the flour. Beat for about 30 seconds until batter is smooth.

5. Divide batter evenly between prepared muffin cups. Bake for 18 to 20 minutes, until a cake tester inserted into the centers comes out clean. Rotate pan halfway through for even baking. Cool for 15 minutes on wire rack. Invert onto rack and cool completely.

for glaze

Whisk confectioners' sugar and orange juice together until smooth and thin enough to pour. Add more sugar or more orange juice as needed. Spoon glaze over top of the inverted cupcakes.

for sugared cranberries

1. Combine sugar and water in a small saucepan over low heat. Stir until sugar completely dissolves. Bring to a simmer and remove from heat. Stir in cranberries and pour into a bowl. Cover and refrigerate for 8 hours or overnight.

2. Drain cranberries in a colander. Place superfine sugar in a shallow bowl. Roll cranberries in the sugar to fully coat. Spread sugared cranberries in a single layer on a parchment-lined baking sheet. Let stand at room temperature for at least 1 hour or until dry.

3. Garnish glazed cupcakes with sugared cranberries and serve.

Pudding Truffles

❄ 40–50 TRUFFLES

PREP TIME: 35 MIN
COOKING TIME: 10 MIN
CHILLING TIME: 2 HR

ingredients ❄ ❄ ❄ ❄ ❄ ❄ ❄ ❄ ❄ ❄

¾ cup (180 ml) heavy cream

4 tablespoons whisky

9 ounces (270 g) dark chocolate, chopped

7 ounces (210 g) milk chocolate, chopped

½ cup (120 g) unsalted butter, room temperature
   (1 stick)

½ cup (65 g) dried fruit, finely chopped

¼ cup (35 g) almond, finely chopped

to decorate

2 cups (240 g) confectioners' sugar

2–3 tablespoons lemon juice

Marzipan leaves and berries

method ❄ ❄ ❄ ❄ ❄ ❄ ❄ ❄ ❄ ❄

1. Bring the cream and whisky to a boil. Remove
from heat and stir in the chocolates. Let rest for
several minutes to melt. Stir until smooth and
creamy. Cool slightly.

2. Using an electric mixer on medium speed,
beat the butter until creamy. Stir butter into the
chocolate cream. Add fruit and almonds. Refrigerate
for 1 hour.

3. Line a baking sheet pan with parchment paper.
Using a teaspoon, shape the mixture into balls and
place on prepared pan.

to decorate

Sift the confectioners' sugar and add lemon juice
1 tablespoon at a time until thin enough to pour.
Drizzle glaze over truffles. Decorate with marzipan
leaves and berries. Refrigerate for 1 hour before
serving.

Ice Cream and Coconut Snowmen

❄ 8 SNOWMEN

PREP TIME: 25 MIN
FREEZER TIME: 30 MIN

ingredients ❄ ❄ ❄ ❄ ❄ ❄ ❄ ❄ ❄ ❄

½ gallon (1.5 kg) premium vanilla ice cream

28 ounces (800 g) flake sweetened coconut

2 tablespoons marzipan

Orange food coloring

2 shoestring black licorice laces, cut into
    small pieces

8 marshmallows, roasted

8 chocolate wafers

Confectioners' sugar

method ❄ ❄ ❄ ❄ ❄ ❄ ❄ ❄ ❄ ❄

1. Line a baking sheet that fits in the freezer with parchment paper. Using 3 different-sized ice cream scoops, make 24 rounded scoops, 8 of each size. Place scoops on the baking sheet and freeze for 15 to 20 minutes to harden slightly.

2. Place flake coconut in a shallow bowl, and roll ice cream in coconut. Place coconut covered scoops on the pan and return to the freezer.

3. Add 1 drop of food coloring at a time to the marzipan until carrot-orange color. Make 8 carrot noses, using a paring knife to make ridges. Remove small scoop of ice cream at a time from the freezer and decorate using licorice pieces for the eyes and mouth and a marzipan carrot for the nose. Return to freezer until ready to serve.

4. Remove 1 middle size scoop of ice cream at a time from the freezer and place licorice pieces down the front to create buttons. Assemble snowmen, lightly pressing scoops together. Return snowmen to the freezer until ready to serve.

5. Make top hats by roasting marshmallows over the flame of a gas burner. Place roasted marshmallows while still hot on top of a chocolate wafer to stick. Dust with confectioners' sugar. Place top hats on snowmen just before serving.

tip: Top hats can also be created using marzipan and black food coloring.

holiday specialties

Blackberry and Raspberry Tart

❄ 6 SERVINGS

PREP TIME: 30 MIN
CHILLING TIME: 1 HR 30 MIN
BAKING TIME: 20–25 MIN

ingredients ❄ ❄ ❄ ❄ ❄ ❄ ❄ ❄ ❄ ❄

for vanilla pastry cream

3 tablespoons sugar
1 tablespoon all-purpose flour
1 tablespoon cornstarch
2 egg yolks
⅔ cup (180 ml) milk
1 teaspoon vanilla

for pastry dough

1 egg yolk
2 tablespoons ice water
1 teaspoon vanilla extract
1¼ cups (150 g) all-purpose flour
⅓ cup (65 g) sugar
¼ teaspoon salt
½ cup (120 g) unsalted butter, cold (1 stick)

2 cups (250 g) blackberries
2 cups (250 g) raspberries

method ❄ ❄ ❄ ❄ ❄ ❄ ❄ ❄ ❄ ❄

for vanilla pastry cream

1. Using an electric mixer set on medium speed, beat sugar, flour, cornstarch and egg yolks together until thick and pale, about 3 minutes.

2. In a saucepan over medium heat, bring the milk and vanilla to a simmer. While stirring, pour half of the hot milk into the sugar mixture, stirring to blend. Pour the sugar and milk mixture back into the pan with the remaining milk. Cook over medium-low heat, stirring constantly, until the mixture thickens. Scrape the sides and bottom of the pan frequently to prevent scorching.

3. Pour the thickened pastry cream into a bowl. Cover the surface with plastic wrap. Cool at room temperature, then refrigerate for at least 1 hour.

for pastry dough

1. In a small bowl, whisk together egg yolk, water and vanilla. Set aside.

2. In a large bowl, stir the flour, sugar and salt together. Cut the butter into small cubes and using two knives or a pastry blender, cut into the flour mixture until the texture resembles breadcrumbs. Add the egg mixture with a fork until the dough sticks together.

3. Shape the dough into a ball and flatten into a disk. Wrap in plastic and refrigerate for about 30 minutes.

to assemble

1. Preheat oven to 400°F (200°C).

2. Lightly flour a work surface. Roll out the pastry dough into an 11-inch (28 cm) round. Transfer dough to a 9-inch (23 cm) tart pan. Trim excess dough so the edges are flush with the rim of the pan. Line the pastry shell with parchment paper and fill with pie weights and bake for 5 minutes.

3. Reduce oven temperature to 350°F (180°C). Remove pie weights and parchment. Prick the bottom of the crust with a fork. Bake until pastry is golden, about 15 to 20 minutes longer. Place on a wire rack and cool for at least 1 hour.

4. Once cool, spoon the vanilla pastry cream into the crust. Arrange fresh berries on top. Serve.

Dark Chocolate Truffles

PREP TIME: 25 MIN
CHILLING TIME: 3 HR
COOKING TIME: 10 MIN

ingredients ❄ ❄ ❄ ❄ ❄ ❄ ❄ ❄ ❄

8 ounces (240 g) bittersweet chocolate, chopped
½ cup (120 ml) heavy cream
2 tablespoons unsalted butter
2 tablespoons brandy or flavored liqueur, optional

coatings for truffles

Dutch-processed cocoa powder, sifted
Confectioners' sugar
Shaved chocolate
Toasted and finely chopped walnuts, pecans
   or almonds
Melted chocolate

30 small paper candy cups

method ❄ ❄ ❄ ❄ ❄ ❄ ❄ ❄ ❄

1. Place the chopped chocolate in a medium heatproof bowl. Set aside.

2. In a small saucepan over medium heat, heat the cream and butter until it just begins to boil. Pour hot mixture over the chocolate and let stand for about 2 minutes. Stir until smooth. Add brandy or liqueur, if using.

3. Cover and place in the refrigerator for at least 3 hours or overnight, until the truffle mixture is firm.

4. Place the various coatings on small plates. When the truffle mixture is firm, use a small spoon to form the chocolate into round bite-sized balls. Roll truffles between lightly-oiled palms to form round balls and then roll in coating of choice. Place on a parchment-lined baking sheet.

5. Cover and refrigerate until firm. Store in an airtight container in the refrigerator up to 2 weeks. May be frozen up to 2 months. Serve in paper candy cups.

Walnut Potica

✳ 2 NUT ROLLS

PREP TIME: 30 MIN
RISING TIME: 13 HR
BAKING TIME: 40–50 MIN

ingredients ✳ ✳ ✳ ✳ ✳ ✳ ✳ ✳ ✳ ✳

for dough

1 package active dry yeast

¼ cup (60 ml) warm water

1 cup (240 g) unsalted butter (2 sticks)

½ cup (120 ml) milk

2 tablespoons sugar

½ teaspoon salt

3 egg yolks, beaten (save whites for filling)

2¼ cups (270 g) all-purpose flour

for filling

1½ cups (180 g) walnuts, finely ground

1 cup (200 g) sugar, divided

1 teaspoon cinnamon

½ teaspoon ground cloves

¼ cup (60 ml) milk

¼ cup (60 ml) honey

3 egg whites

1 tablespoon fresh lemon zest

1 cup (145 g) raisins

2 tablespoons unsalted butter, melted

method ✳ ✳ ✳ ✳ ✳ ✳ ✳ ✳ ✳ ✳

for dough

1. Dissolve yeast in warm water 110°F (45°C) and set aside. In a small saucepan over medium heat, melt butter, milk, sugar and salt together until milk is warm.

2. In a large bowl, combine yeast mixture, butter mixture, and beaten egg yolks. Gradually add the flour, beating until dough is smooth. Divide the dough into 2 equal portions, wrap in plastic wrap and refrigerate overnight.

for filling

1. In a saucepan over low heat, combine walnuts, ¼ cup (50 g) sugar, cinnamon, cloves, milk and honey. Stir constantly until sugar is dissolved and mixture is hot. Remove from heat and let cool.

2. Beat egg whites until light and frothy. Gradually add remaining sugar and beat until stiff peaks form. Gently fold egg whites and lemon zest into cooled walnut mixture. Set aside.

3. On a lightly floured surface, roll dough into a square ¼-inch (.5 cm) thick. Spread nut mixture over dough and sprinkle evenly with raisins. Roll into a log.

4. Place nut rolls in well-greased loaf pans. Pierce the tops in several places with a fork. Cover pans with clean kitchen towels and set aside in a warm place to rise for about 1 hour.

5. Preheat oven to 350°F (180°C).

6. Bake rolls for 40 to 50 minutes. Brush tops with melted butter during the last 15 minutes of baking. Cool rolls in the pan for 10 minutes on a wire rack. Loosen edges with a knife and turn rolls out onto rack. Serve warm or at room temperature.

Julbullar Swedish Sweet Rolls

PREP TIME: 1 HR 20 MIN
RISING TIME: 1 HR
BAKING TIME: 20 MIN

ingredients ✳ ✳ ✳ ✳ ✳ ✳ ✳ ✳ ✳ ✳

for dough

2 cups (480 ml) milk
2 packets active dry yeast
½ cup (100 g) sugar, divided
½ teaspoon salt
1 teaspoon ground cardamom
4½ cups (660 g) all-purpose flour

for filling

½ cup (120 g) unsalted butter, softened (1 stick)
2 tablespoons sugar
1 teaspoon vanilla extract
1 tablespoon cinnamon
2 teaspoons pumpkin pie spice
½ cup (160 g) cranberry jam

for egg wash

1 large egg
2 tablespoons milk

Colored sugar pearls

method ✳ ✳ ✳ ✳ ✳ ✳ ✳ ✳ ✳ ✳

1. Heat milk until just warm 110°F (45°C). Remove from heat, add yeast and 1 tablespoon sugar. Stir and let rest for 5 minutes.

2. In a large mixing bowl, combine milk and yeast mixture with salt, sugar, cardamom and just enough flour to make a smooth, elastic dough. Cover with plastic wrap and let rise in a warm place until doubled in size, about 30 minutes.

3. For filling: In a small bowl, cream the butter, sugar, vanilla and spices together. Set aside.

4. Punch dough down, knead, and add more flour as needed to prevent sticking. On a lightly floured surface, roll out dough into a large rectangle about ½-inch (1 cm) thick.

4. Spread spiced butter to within ½ inch (1 cm) of dough edges. Spread with a thin layer of cranberry jam. Roll from the long side of the rectangle jellyroll style. Press edges together to seal. Cut into slices about ¾-inch (2 cm) wide. Place on a baking sheet lined with parchment paper. Cover and let rise in a warm place about 30 minutes or until doubled in size.

6. Preheat the oven to 375°F (190°C).

7. Whisk egg and milk together. Brush rolls with egg wash and sprinkle with sugar pearls. Bake for about 20 minutes, until golden brown. Cool on a wire rack and serve.

Glazed Walnut Stollen

❄ 16 SERVINGS

PREP TIME: 30 MIN
RISING TIME: 2 HR
BAKING TIME: 15–20 MIN

ingredients ❄ ❄ ❄ ❄ ❄ ❄ ❄ ❄ ❄ ❄

1 package active dry yeast
1 cup (240 ml) warm milk
½ cup (120 g) unsalted butter, softened (1 stick)
½ cup (100 g) sugar
2 large eggs, room temperature
1 teaspoon salt
4¼ cups (500 g) all-purpose flour, plus extra
3 cups (360 g) walnuts, finely chopped
1 cup (220 g) brown sugar, packed
2 tablespoons light cream
1 tablespoon vanilla extract
2 teaspoons cinnamon

for glaze

1½ cups (180 g) confectioners' sugar
1 teaspoon vanilla extract
1–2 tablespoons milk
¼ cup (30 g) walnuts, finely chopped

method ❄ ❄ ❄ ❄ ❄ ❄ ❄ ❄ ❄ ❄

1. In a large bowl, dissolve yeast in warm milk 110°F (45°C). Let rest for 5 minutes. Add butter, sugar, eggs, salt and 2 cups (240 g) of flour. Using an electric mixer on low speed, beat until smooth.

2. Stir in enough of the remaining flour to form a soft and pliable dough. On a lightly floured surface, knead dough until smooth and elastic, about 6 to 8 minutes. Place dough in a greased bowl, turning to coat completely. Cover with plastic wrap and let rise in a warm place until doubled in size, about 1¼ hours.

3. Punch dough down and divide in half. Roll out into 2 rectangles.

4. In a large bowl, combine chopped walnuts, brown sugar, cream, vanilla and cinnamon. Spread nut filling down the middle of each stollen. Roll from the long side to within 1 inch (2.5 cm) of the opposite side, jellyroll style. Press edges together to seal.

5. Place on a greased baking sheet. Cover and let rise for 45 minutes or until nearly doubled.

6. Preheat oven to 350°F (180°C). Using a sharp knife or bread-slashing tool, make 8 slashes across the top of the unbaked loaf. Bake for 15 to 20 minutes or until golden brown. Cool on wire racks.

for glaze

In a small bowl, combine confectioners' sugar, vanilla and enough milk to make a thin glaze. Drizzle glaze over the top and sprinkle with finely chopped walnuts. Serve.

Gift Fruit Cakes

❄ 6 CAKES

PREP TIME: 20 MIN
BAKING TIME: 20–25 MIN

ingredients ✳ ✳ ✳ ✳ ✳ ✳ ✳ ✳ ✳ ✳

½ cup (75 g) mixed dried fruits

1½ cups (180 g) all-purpose flour

1 teaspoon baking powder

½ teaspoon ground allspice

¼ teaspoon salt

10 tablespoons (180 g) unsalted butter, softened (1¼ sticks)

¾ cup (150 g) sugar

1 teaspoon vanilla extract

2 large eggs, room temperature

½ cup (120 ml) milk

Confectioners' sugar

Decorative candies

method ✳ ✳ ✳ ✳ ✳ ✳ ✳ ✳ ✳ ✳

1. Preheat the oven to 375°F (190°C). Spray the pan with baking spray or grease and dust lightly with flour, tapping out any excess.

2. Chop dried fruits coarsely and toss with 1 tablespoon flour to prevent sticking.

3. In a bowl, sift flour, baking powder, allspice and salt together. Set aside.

4. Using an electric mixer on medium speed, beat butter and sugar together until smooth and creamy, about 4 minutes. Add vanilla. Beat in 1 egg at a time, mixing well.

5. Gradually stir in flour mixture and milk. Pour half the batter into the pan. Distribute dried fruit on top and cover with remaining batter.

6. Bake for 20 to 25 min. Cool in the pan for 10 minutes on a wire rack. Invert cakes onto rack and cool completely.

7. Decorate with confectioners' sugar and candies.

[BAKED IN THE NORDIC WARE PRETTY PRESENTS PAN]

holiday specialties

Meringue Rosettes with Coffee Cream

❄ 36 COOKIES

PREP TIME: 15 MIN
BAKING TIME: 2 HR–2 HR 30 MIN

ingredients ✳ ✳ ✳ ✳ ✳ ✳ ✳ ✳ ✳

for meringues

2 egg whites
¼ teaspoon salt
1 cup (120 g) confectioners' sugar

for coffee cream filling

½ cup (120 ml) heavy cream
1 teaspoon vanilla extract
2 tablespoons instant coffee
4½ ounces (130 g) white chocolate, chopped

method ✳ ✳ ✳ ✳ ✳ ✳ ✳ ✳ ✳

for meringues

1. Preheat oven to 175°F (80°C). Line a baking sheet with parchment paper.

2. In a large bowl, beat the egg whites and salt with an electric mixer on medium-high speed until soft peaks form. Slowly add the confectioners' sugar and continue beating until the peaks are firm and glossy.

3. Spoon the meringue into a pastry bag fitted with a plain tip. Using half of the meringue, pipe solid circles 1¼ inch (3 cm) in diameter for the bases onto the prepared baking sheet. Use the remaining meringue to pipe rosettes for the tops. You will have 36 of each.

4. Bake for 2 to 2½ hours. Do not brown. When the meringues are dry, remove from oven and cool on a wire rack.

for coffee cream filling

1. Place the cream, vanilla and instant coffee in a saucepan over medium-high heat. Bring the mixture to a boil.

2. Remove from heat, stir in the chopped chocolate and continue stirring until the chocolate has melted. Cool slightly, then refrigerate.

3. Beat chilled coffee cream until smooth and creamy. Spoon into pastry bag fitted with a plain tip. Pipe cream onto the meringue base and top with a rosette. Serve.